1-15-73

GOETHE.

GOETHE

His Life and Writings

BY

OSCAR BROWNING, M.A.

Fellow of King's College, Cambridge

LONDON

SWAN SONNENSCHEIN & CO.

NEW YORK: MACMILLAN & CO.

1892

HASKELL HOUSE PUBLISHERS Ltd.

Publishers of Scarce Scholarly Books

NEW YORK. N. Y. 10012

1972

HASKELL HOUSE PUBLISHERS Lᴛᴅ.

Publishers of Scarce Scholarly Books

280 LAFAYETTE STREET

NEW YORK. N. Y. 10012

Library of Congress Cataloging in Publication Data

Browning, Oscar, 1837-1923.
    Goethe: his life and writings.

    Reprint of the 1892 ed., which was issued as no. 5 of
The Dilettante library.
    Bibliography: p.
    1. Goethe, Johann Wolfgang von, 1749-1852--Biography.
I. Title. II. Series: The Dilettante library, 5.
PT2049.B7 1972   831'.6 [B]   72-2126
ISBN 0-8383-1493-7

Printed in the United States of America

PREFACE.

THIS account of Goethe's life and writings is reprinted, with alterations and additions, from an article contributed to the last edition of the "Encyclopædia Britannica." It is possible that the discoveries of the last ten years may not have been completely represented in this revision ; but it is difficult to alter much in what has been carefully conceived and planned without injuriously affecting the harmony and balance of the whole, and the desirability of preserving this has been constantly before the writer's mind.

[*Reprinted, by permission of* Messrs. A. and C. BLACK, *from the* "ENCYCLOPÆDIA BRITANNICA," *with additions by the Author.*]

CONTENTS.

GOETHE.

JOHANN WOLFGANG VON GOETHE (1749–1832) was born in Frankfort on August 28, 1749. His parents were citizens of that Imperial town, and Wolf gang was their only son and their eldest child. His father was born on July 31, 1710, and in 1742 received the title of Imperial Councillor. He married on August 20, 1748, at the age of thirty-eight, Catherine Elizabeth Textor, a girl of seventeen. Her family was better than his own, and held a higher position in the town. Her father was imperial councillor, and had been schul-theiss, or chief magistrate. In Decem-

ber, 1750, was born a daughter, Cornelia,
who remained until her death, at the age
of twenty-seven, her brother's most intimate friend. She was married in 1773
to John George Schlosser. The house
in which Goethe was born is still to be
seen in the Hirschgraben. Goethe has
described to us how it was rebuilt, and
it has since been much altered. His
education was irregular ; he went to no
school, and his father rather stimulated
than instructed him. But the atmo-
sphere by which he was surrounded gave
him, perhaps, the best education he
could have received. Frankfort, a free
town of the Empire, still preserved the
appearance of the Middle Ages. It had
lost the reality of power, but its citizens
naturally grew up with a strong sense of
independence, and a power of realizing
the unity of Germany which was want-
ing in a small State. The boy from his
earliest youth was accustomed to the

companionship of his elders. His father was strict and formal, his mother quick and lively, inspired with no small share of the genius of her son. Goethe lived in the freest intercouise with every kind of society in the town, in which he might expect some day to be an important personage. There was no capital like London or Paris to call him away from the provinces; Berlin was poor and distant, Vienna half Italian and half Spanish. Goethe must have been brought up with the ambition to take his degree at the university as doctor, to return home and become an advocate, to make a rich marriage, to go through the regular course of civil offices, to inherit his father's house, and perhaps one day to be burgomaster. His home was a cultivated one. The father was fond of art and of the German poetry then in fashion. The influence of Lessing had scarcely made itself felt; Herder was

only five years older than Goethe himself. Gellert and Gottsched were the two
oracles of poetry,—Gottsched a pedantic
product of the earlier French culture,
Gellert old-fashioned and immovable, and
unable to comprehend the new spirit.
The chief debt that Goethe owed to
him was the improvement in his hand-
writing, on which Gellert laid great
stress, and which he coupled with moral
excellence. Goethe's father had a great
respect for these rhyming poets, and he
so strongly objected to the new German
hexameters that Wolfgang could only
read Klopstock's *Messiah* with his sister
in the greatest secrecy and in terror of
discovery. He did, however, read it,
and learned much of it by heart. French
culture gave at this time the prevailing
tone to Europe. Goethe could not have
escaped its influence, and he was destined to fall under it in a special manner.
In the Seven Years' War, which was

then raging, France took the side of the
Empire against Frederick the Great.
Frankfort was full of French soldiers,
and a certain Comte Thorane, who was
quartered in Goethe's house, had an
important influence on the boy. Still
more strongly was he affected by the
French company of actors, whom he
came to know both on and off the
stage. He learned to declaim in this
manner passages of Racine without
understanding a word of them. At a
later period he knew French thoroughly
well, and wrote both prose and poetry in
that language. His first writings were
imitations of the French manner; his
earliest play was the imitation of a
French after-piece. We can understand
how these different forces were to work
upon his future life. From his father
he derived the steadfastness of character
which enabled him to pursue an indepen-
dent career of self-culture and devotion

to Art in the midst of every kind of distracting influence; from his mother he inherited the joyous nature and lively sympathy, the flow of language and love of narration, without which he could not have been a poet. Before the age of sixteen he had seen every kind of life in a city particularly favourable to a richness of individual character; he was entirely free from the prejudices of a small State; and as far as he cared for Germany he cared for it as a whole. He was tinged at an early age with the influence of the clearest and most finished language in Europe; and this influence, uniting with similar qualities in Goethe's mind, made his prose a new phenomenon in the literature of his country, unlike anything which had been seen before. Lastly, with the most passionate aspirations for freedom and independence of life, he was born into the slavery of a mechanical career of prosaic prosperity, the pressure of which was not strong enough to confine him, but was strong enough to stimulate all his efforts to break the bonds.

Goethe, if we may believe his auto-biography, experienced his first love about the age of fifteen in the person of Gretchen, whom some have supposed to be the daughter of an innkeeper at Offenbach. He worshipped her as Dante worshipped Beatrice. She treated him as a child, much as Miss Chaworth treated Byron. But there is no other evidence of this first love, and it would be quite in accordance with Goethe's manner to enlarge on a very small foundation, or to concentrate on one person the feelings which were devoted to several individuals. His letters speak of a boyish love for one Charitas Meixner, a friend of his sister, two years younger than himself, the daughter of a rich merchant at Worms.

First love.

He expresses his affection for her with all the fervour of French phraseology, and the passion did not leave him when he had removed to Leipsic. But Charitas was able to console herself with another engagement. She married in February, 1773, a merchant of her native town, and died at the end of the following year.

Leipsic.   In the autumn of 1765 Goethe, who had just completed his sixteenth year, travelled to Leipsic in the company of a bookseller, Fleischer, and his wife, who were on tneir way to attend the fair. On the 19th of October he was admitted as a student of the Bavarian nation, one of the four into which the University was divided. For his lodging he had two neat little rooms in the Feuerkugel, the Fire Ball, looking into the long court-yard which leads from the old market to the new. When we remember that his three years at Leipsic, about which so much has been written, correspond with the last three years of an English boy at a public school, we can form some idea of the singular individuality of his character and the maturity and ripeness of his genius. He was sent to Leipsic to study law, in order that he might return to Frankfort fitted for the regular course of municipal distinction. For this purpose he carried with him a letter to Professor Böhme, who taught history and public law in the University, but had no other distinction to recommend him. He told Professor Böhme that he intended to devote himself, not to law, but to *belles lettres*, or, to use the word which F. A. Wolf had invented, philology. Böhme did his best to dissuade him, and in this was assisted by his wife. The effect of their advice was rather to disgust Goethe with modern German literature, to make him despise what he had already written,

and to drive him into the distractions of
society, which wasted both his time and
his money. He did, however, attend
some lectures. He heard the lectures
of Ernesti on Cicero's *Orator*, but the
professor dealt rather with questions of
grammar than of taste. He attended
Gellert's lectures on literature, and even
joined his private class.

Gellert held a high position among
German men of letters, which was due
quite as much to his character as to his
genius. He advised Goethe to desert
poetry for prose, and to take to authorship only as an employment subordinate
to the serious occupations of his life.
Goethe tells us that in his lectures upon
taste he never heard Gellert mention the
names of Klopstock, Kleist, Wieland,
Gessner, Gleim, or Lessing. He also
attended the lectures of another literary
professor, Clodius, a young man about
ten years older than himself. Clodius

corrected Goethe's writings with red ink,
and pointed out the faults without showing the way to mend them. Goethe
had written a poem of congratulation
for the marriage of his uncle Textor
(February 17th, 1766), which, according
to the fashion of the time, was full of
gods and goddesses and other mytho-
logical apparatus. Clodius was unspar-
ingly hard upon this production, and
Goethe then perceived that his critic
was just as faulty as himself in the use
of abstractions and strange outlandish
words to give weight and authority to his
verse. He satirized Clodius by writing a
poem in praise of the cakes of the con-
fectioner Händel, and by a parody of
his drama *Medon.* His position towards
the professors of his University was not
an enviable one. His real University
education was derived from intercourse
with his friends. First among these
was J. G. Schlosser, who afterwards

married his sister. Goethe used to dine
with him at a *table d'hôte* kept by a
wine-dealer, Schönkopf, in the Bruhl
(No. 79), in a house which still exists.
Schlosser, who was at this time private
secretary to the duke of Würtemberg
and tutor to his children, was ten years
older than Goethe. He had a great
influence upon him, chiefly in intro-
ducing him to a wider circle of German,
French, English, and Italian poetry.
At the table of Professor Ludwig, where
Goethe had previously dined, the conversation had generally turned on medical and scientific subjects. Another
friend of Goethe's was Behrisch, tutor
to the young Count Lindenau. He was
a man in middle life, and he combined
originality of character and clearness of
literary judgment with a dry and caus-
tic wit, and an ever-abiding sense of
humour, much in the same proportions
as were found in Merck, who exercised

at a later period an important influence
over Goethe's career. His friendship
with Goethe was not at first of advan-
tage to him. He was deprived of his
tutorship from a suspicion that he did
not always keep the most select society,
and his successor was forbidden to allow
his charge to associate with the young
poet. This is supposed to have been
caused by Goethe's disrespectful be-
haviour to Professor Clodius. Gellert
obtained for Behrisch an educational
post at the court of Dessau, and Goethe
kept up a constant correspondence with
him till his death in 1809. Behrisch
would not allow Goethe to print his
poems, but copied them out instead in a
beautiful hand. He probably had a considerable effect in producing the simplicity
and naturalness of Goethe's early style.

But the person who had the strongest Oeser.
effect on Goethe's mental development
was Adam Frederick Oeser, at this time

director of the Academy of Arts in Leipsic. Goethe took lessons from him in
drawing, and, not content with this, tried
his hand at etching. A little device of
his for a book-plate or a bill-head is
extant, in which a slab with the name
C. G. Schönkopf is represented with
three bottles above and a wreath of
flowers below. Oeser had been a friend
of Winckelmann's, and exercised great
influence over his views of Art. This
was a source of considerable reputation
to him, and Winckelmann's tragic death,
the news of which reached Leipsic whilst
Goethe was there, must have brought
the relation between them into stronger
relief. Goethe always spoke of Oeser's
influence with the greatest affection and
respect. He writes—" Oeser's discoveries have given me a fresh opportunity of blessing myself that I had him
for my instructor. He entered into our
very souls, and we must indeed have

been without souls not to have derived benefit from him. His lessons will produce their effects through all the rest of my existence. He taught me that the ideal of beauty is simplicity and repose." We find Goethe at Weimar continually consulting Oeser for designs for furniture and for theatrical entertainments.

Goethe from his earliest years was never without a passion, and at Leipsic his passion was Kitty Schönkopf, the Aennchen of the autobiography, the daughter of the host at whose house he dined. She often teased him with her inconstant ways, and to this experience is due his first drama *Die Laune des Verliebten,* "Lovers' Quarrels," as it may be styled. It is a mere trifle, a pastoral in one act, written in alexandrines in the French style. Two happy and two unhappy lovers are contrasted. The only interest of the piece is, that it is a fragment from Goethe's own life.

Käthchen Schön-kopf.

A deeper chord is struck in *Die Mit-schuldigen* (The Fellow-Sinners), which forms a dismal and forbidding picture both of the time and of the experiences of the youth who wrote it. The daughter of an innkeeper has made an unhappy marriage, and is visited by a former lover who is in good circumstances. An assignation is arranged, and the inter-view is witnessed by the husband, who has come to steal the stranger's purse. The father comes in to read one of the stranger's letters. He is surprised, and is with his daughter suspected of the theft. The real culprit is discovered, but defends himself by accusing the stranger of his conduct to his wife. So they are all guilty. This play was first written in one act. It was afterwards enlarged to three acts, and published in 1787. The manuscript, which still exists, was given to Frederike Brion of Sesen-heim. Besides these plays Goethe wrote

at Leipsic twenty little songs of an erotic
character, which were set to music by
his young friend Breitkopf.   He describes them as moral-sensuous, but they
are more sensuous than moral.   They
have the merit of a musical easy flow
of expression, various moods of passion,
with a happy readiness and elegance.
Only a few of them were included in his
collected works, and those very much
altered.   They show the influence of
Wieland ; but by one side of Wieland
Goethe was never affected.   He was
never led to mingle classical ideas and
emblems with the unrestrained and
sensual frivolity which was disseminated
from France.   He never imitated Aga-
thon or Musarion.   Whatever may have
been the bitterness of his experience of
life, or the waywardness of his excited
fancy, he conceived a true idea of the
real nature of classical Art.   In this
Winckelmann and Lessing were his

teachers, and he was never untrue to the
lessons which they inculcated.   This was
the most valuable possession he brought
back from Leipsic.   He had an opportunity of establishing his principles of
taste during a short visit to Dresden, in
which he devoted himself to the pictures
and the antiques.   The end of Goethe's
stay at Leipsic was saddened by illness.
One morning at the beginning of the
summer he was awakened by a violent
hemorrhage.   For several days he hung
between life and death, and after that
his recovery was slow, although he was
tended with the greatest anxiety by his
friends.   He finally left Leipsic far from
well on August 28, 1768, his nineteenth
birthday.

Frankfort.   Goethe made an enforced stay of a
year and a half in his native town.   It
was perhaps the least happy part of his
life.   He was in bad health.   His cure
proceeded slowly, and he had several

relapses, and the weakness of the lungs, which was his first complaint, was succeeded by a weakness of the digestion, which was yet more troublesome and painful. The society of Frankfort seemed to him far less agreeable than that of Leipsic ; he contrasted the cold, stiff, formal, old-fashioned life of the Imperial city with the freshness, geniality, and intellectual activity of the Saxon university. His family relations were not pleasant. His grandfather Textor was struck with paralysis ; his father showed but little sympathy with his aspirations for universal culture, and could imagine no career for him but that of a successful jurist. His sister had grown somewhat harsh and cold during his absence, and was possessed by a morbid self-consciousness, which she committed to the confidential pages of a secret diary. The tone of this diary, partly the result of family temperament,

partly of the character of the age, throws
an interesting light on the despair of
Werther. Goethe's mother was always
the same to him, a bright, genial, sympathetic friend. But her love could not
ward off the pressure of circumstances,
or supply a substitute for a wider and
more unfettered life. Goethe, during
his illness, received great attention from
Fräulein von Klettenberg, a friend of
his mother's, a pietist of the Moravian
school. She initiated him into the
mystical writings of those abstracted
saints, and she engaged him in the study
of alchemy, which served at once to
prepare him for the conception of *Faust*
and for the scientific researches of his
later days. During his stay at Frank
fort he wrote very little. It may be that
the two Leipsic dramas received here
their completed form. A farce in mem
mory of his Leipsic life, a poetical letter
to Frederike Oeser, the daughter of his

teacher, a few songs, some of them religious, make up the tale of his produc-
tions, as far as we know them.

He arrived at Strasburg April 2, Strasburg.
1770. It was intended that after a
sojourn in the University of that place
he should visit Paris, the centre of re-
finement. Goethe stayed in Strasburg
till August 28, 1771, his twenty-second
birthday, and these sixteen months are
perhaps the most important of his life.
During them he came into active con-
tact with most of those impulses of which
his after life was a development. If we
would understand his mental growth, we
must ask who were his friends. He
took his meals at the house of the Fräulein Lauth in the Krämergasse. The
table was mainly filled with medical
students. At the head of it sat Salz-·
mann, a grave man of fifty years of age.
His experience and his refined taste
were very attractive to Goethe, who

made him his intimate friend. Goethe
was soon drawn by the studies of his
companions to desert his own. A note-
book of this date is preserved, which
gives us a full account of his studies and
employments. He attended lectures on
anatomy, on midwifery, and on chemistry.
His own studies were chiefly devoted to
the last science ; and he did not forget
his favourite alchemy. He had brought
with him to Strasburg introductions to
pietistic circles, and this made him at
first somewhat staid and retired in his
pleasures, and disinclined for general
society. This soon wore off, and the
natural cheerfulness of his genial nature
returned to him. Two songs, *Blinde
Kuh* and *Stirbt der Fuchs so gilt der
Balg*, refer to the social life of this
period. He went on picnics, he wrote
French poetry, he took dancing lessons,
he learnt the violoncello. The table of
the Fräulein Lauth received some new

guests. Among these was Jung-Stilling,
the self-educated charcoal-burner, who
in his memoir has left a graphic account
of Goethe's striking appearance, his
broad brow, his flashing eye, his mas-
tery of the company, and his generosity
of character. Another was Lerse, a
frank open character who became
Goethe's favourite, and whose name is
immortalized in *Götz von Berlichingen*.
Goethe did not desert his studies in Art.
He learnt from the constant study of the
cathedral of Strasburg the effect of
Gothic architecture, and he shuddered
when he saw the reception-rooms of the
youthful Marie Antoinette hung with
tapestries which represented the marriage of Jason and Medea, and seemed
to forebode the coming doom. His
diary also shows that he spent much
time in philosophical speculation. But
the most important event of his Strasburg sojourn was his acquaintance with

Herder. Herder was five years older than Goethe. He was then travelling as tutor to the young prince of Holstein-Eutin, but was obliged to spend the whole winter of 1770–71 in Strasburg on account of an affection of his eyes Goethe was with him every day, often all day. Herder, who was a pupil of a more original genius, Hamann, taught him the true value of Nature in Art, and the principles of what we should now call the romantic school. He made *Ossian* known to him, and the wealth of popular poetry in all nations which the publication of *Ossian* revealed ; he enchanted him with the idyllic simplicity of the *Vicar of Wakefield ;* but, above all, he shook Goethe's sensibility to the roots by revealing to him the power of the mighty Shakespeare. He now saw how far superior Homer was to his Latin imitators, and how false were the canons of French Art. Goethe's spirit was liberated from its trammels, and *Götz* and *Faust* and *Wilhelm Meister* became possible to his mind. At a later period he forged for himself fetters of a different kind.

Goethe's stay at Strasburg is generally connected still more closely with another circumstance,—his passion for Frederike Brion of Sesenheim. The village lies about twenty miles from Strasburg, and Frederike's father was pastor there. Goethe was introduced by his friend Weyland, an Alsatian, as a poor theological student. Fresh from his study of Goldsmith, he found the *Vicar of Wakefield* realized. The father was a simple worthy man, the eldest of the three daughters was married, the two younger remained, — Maria Salome, whom Goethe calls Olivia, and Frederike, to whom the poet principally devoted himself. She was tall and slight, with fair hair and blue eyes, and just

Sesenheim.

sixteen years of age. Goethe gave him
self up to the passion of the moment ;
what he felt and suffered is known to us
by his songs. At least ten songs are
addressed to her, and several others were
written for her. During the winter of
1770, in the intervals of his conversations
with Herder, Goethe often rode over to
Sesenheim. Neither storm, nor cold, nor
darkness kept him back. He should have
been busy with his dissertation for the
degree of doctor. The subject he had
chosen was the duty of providing an
established Church. But the attractions
of Frederike were a great interruption to
his labours. In the spring Herder went
away. The fine weather drew Goethe
still more strongly to Sesenheim. Picnics, water parties, games, dances, and
other amusements, illuminated by enthusiasm for literature, filled up the weeks.
As his time for leaving Strasburg came
nearer, he felt that this love was merely

a dream, and could have no serious termination. Frederike felt the same on her side. A visit of the mother and daughters to Strasburg in July made this appear more clearly. On August 6 Goethe took his degree as doctor of law. Shortly afterwards he bade adieu to Sesenheim, and the tears stood in Frederike's eyes as he reached out his hand from horseback. From Frankfort he wrote his final farewell ; and it was then, as he tells us, that he found from her answer for the first time how deeply she had loved him. The account of this love episode in the autobiography does Goethe injustice. There is nothing in the letters or the poems of the time to show that he had wantonly trifled with her affections. Eight years afterwards, on his way to Switzerland, he spent a night with the Brions at Sesenheim, and was received with the utmost kindness. He was shown the arbour where he had sat, the songs he had written, the carriage he had painted. He left them in the morning with content. Frederike lived till 1813, well known for her works of charity. She never married; the heart that Goethe had loved, she said, should never love another.

Return to Frankfort. Goethe's return to Frankfort is marked by a number of songs, of which the "Wanderer's Sturmlied" is the most remarkable. He found his Frankfort existence more intolerable than before. He had outgrown many of the friends of his youth. Those with whom he felt most sympathy were the two Schlossers and his sister Cornelia. He found in her alone one who sympathized with all his aspirations. He cared nothing for his profession; he was more determined than ever to devote himself to letters, and not to law. He found in the neighbouring town of Darmstadt a literary circle which Frankfort did not supply. The land-

gravine Caroline set a good example,
and had collected round her a number
of kindred spirits, men and women.
Among them were Wenck, and Peter-
sen, and Caroline Flachsland, who was
afterwards to marry Herder. But the
soul of the literary circle was Merck,
now thirty years of age, attached to the
War Office. Goethe has represented
him in the autobiography as a cold and
unfeeling cynic, a spirit who always
said No, a prototype of Mephistopheles.
History represents him otherwise as a
man of cultivated and chastened judg
ment, a represser of enthusiasm, a re-
specter of the rules of Art, anxious to
hold the balance between the old school
and the new. Goethe had dominated
over all his other friends ; Merck dominated over him. He has left but little
of his own writings. He was one of
those who inspire genius in others, and
whose truest picture lives in the recol-

lections of their friends. These months
were full of literary activity. To them
belong an oration on Shakespeare, de-
livered at Frankfort, an essay on Erwin
von Steinbach, the builder of the Strasburg cathedral, two theological treatises
of a neologistic character on the com-
mandments of Moses and the miraculous
tongues of Pentecost, and a number of
reviews written for the *Frankfurter
Gelehrte Anzeiger*, which had been
founded by Merck. But the work into
which he threw all his genius was the
dramatization of the history of the Imperial knight of the Middle Ages, Gott-

*Götz von
Berlich-
ingen.*
fried or Götz von Berlichingen. The
immediate cause of this enterprise was
his enthusiasm for Shakespeare. After
reading him, he felt, he said, like a blind
man who suddenly receives his sight.
The unities of time and place vanished
into nothing. The true form of Art was
seen to be that which holds the wayward

impulses together by an invisible bond,
just as, in the life of man, necessity is
wedded to free will. The study of a
dry and dull biography of Götz, published in 1731, supplied the subject for
his awakened powers. From this miser-
able sketch he conceived within his
mind a complete picture of Germany in
the 16th century. The chief characters
of his play are creatures of his imagination representing the principal types
which made up the history of the time.
Every personage is made to live; they
speak in short sharp sentences like the
powerful lines of a great master's drawing. The first sketch of *Götz* was
finished in six weeks, in the autumn
of 1771. Cornelia was consulted at
every stage in the work. Herder saw
it, and gave his approval. On his
return from Wetzlar, in 1773, Goethe
wrote the piece over again, and published it, with the help of Merck, in the

form in which we now possess it. It ran
like wild-fire through the whole of Germany. It was the progenitor, not only
of the "Sturm und Drang" period to
which it gave the tone, but of the romantic knightly literature which teemed
from the German press. At a later
period, in 1804, Goethe prepared another
edition for the stage, which took five
hours in acting. This recension has
not been represented since.

With the manuscript of *Götz* in his
Wetzlar. pocket, Goethe left Frankfort in the
spring of 1772 for Wetzlar, a quiet country town on the Lahn, one of the seats
of government of the Holy Roman Empire. The emperors lived at Vienna;
they were crowned at Frankfort; they
held their parliaments at Ratisbon, and
at Wetzlar their courts of justice. It
was the custom for young lawyers to
attend the sittings of these courts for a
certain time before they could be ad-

mitted to practise on their own account.
The company of these students, of the
embassies from the component parts of
the Empire, and of various Imperial officials, made the society a pleasant and
lively one.

Goethe soon found friends. The
secretary of the Brunswick legation,
Goué, formed a round table of knights,
—a *Ritter-tafel.* The members adopted
names from the age of chivalry, and ap-
portioned among themselves the neighbouring villages as commanderies and
fiefs. Goethe took the name of Götz.
Deeds of knightly prowess were performed in friendly rivalry, but they
consisted chiefly of eating and drink-
ing. This masquerade at least served
to keep the idea of Götz constantly before Goethe's mind. But the place has
sadder associations. It is impossible
to dissociate the name of Wetzlar from
that of Werther. The Deutsches Haus,

D

then the property of the knights of the
Teutonic Order, exists still in the main
street of Wetzlar. It was occupied by
one of the officials of the Order, by name
Buff, an honest man with a large family
of children. The second daughter,
Lotte, blue-eyed, fair, just twenty years
of age, was first met by Goethe shortly
after his arrival, at a ball at Wolperts-
hausen. She strongly attracted him ; he
became a constant visitor at the house.
He found that Lotte was a second
mother to her brothers and sisters, and
he delighted to play games with them
and tell them stories. Lotte was really
though not formally engaged to Kestner,
a man of two-and-thirty, secretary to
the Hanoverian legation. The discovery
of this relation made no difference to
Goethe ; he remained the devoted friend
of both. He visited Lotte and her
children ; he walked with Kestner about
the streets till midnight ; they kept their
common birthday together in the Ger-

Lotte Buff.

man house on the 28th of August;
Kestner felt no jealousy; Goethe was
content with Lotte's friendship; her
heart was large enough for both. But
the position was too critical to last. On
September 10th they met in the German house for the last time. Lotte
spoke of the other world, and of the
possibility of returning from it. It was
arranged between them that whoever
died first should appear to the others.
This conversation confirmed Goethe's
purpose; he determined to go away.
He made no adieu, but wrote a line to
Kestner to say that he could not have
borne to stay a moment longer. Merck
had probably persuaded him to this step.
To divert his mind he took him to
Ehrenbreitstein and introduced him to
Sophie la Roche, the friend of Wieland's
youth, and to her daughter Maximiliane,
with whom Goethe was charmed. The
most interesting places in the neighbourhood of Coblentz were visited. Goethe

returned to Frankfort by the river in a
yacht.   Here he was possessed with the
memory of Lotte.   He fastened her sil-
houette over his bed.   Kestner came to
Frankfort in September ; Goethe and
Schlosser went together to Wetzlar in
November.   Here he heard of the death
of Jerusalem, a young man attached to
the Brunswick legation.   Goethe had
been with him at the University of Leipsic, but had seen little of him at Wetzlar.
Of a moody temperament, disheartened
by failure in his profession, and soured
by a hopeless passion for the wife of
another, Jerusalem had borrowed a pair
of pistols from Kestner under pretence
of a journey, and had shot himself on
the night of October 29th.

Goethe obtained a full narrative of the
circumstances from Kestner, and im-
Werther. mediately afterwards began his *Werther*,
in which the circumstances above related
are interwoven.   Goethe tells us that it

was written in four weeks, but this can
hardly have been the case. We have
notices of its slow progress during the
whole of the summer of 1773. In 1774
it is far advanced enough to be shown
to some intimate friends. It is not till
the middle of September, 1774, that
two copies of the book are sent in the
greatest secrecy to Sophie la Roche and
Lotte Buff. In October it spread over
the whole of Germany. It was enthusi-
astically praised or sternly condemned.
It was printed, imitated, translated into
every language of Europe, criticized in
every periodical, with the fullest meed of
praise or scorn. It made the round of
the world, and penetrated even to China.
The *Werther* fever wrung the hearts of
men and women with imaginary sorrows;
floods of tears were shed ; young men
dressed in blue coats and yellow breeches
shot themselves with *Werther* in their
hands. It opened the floodgates of pent-

up sentimentalism which had been stirred
by the philosophy of the time, and which
the calamities of the next generation
were sternly to suppress. It may be
imagined that Kestner and Lotte were
not well satisfied with the liberty which
Goethe had taken with their personalities.
They were married on April 4th, 1773,
and Goethe provided the wedding ring.
Notwithstanding the coolness which the
publication of *Werther* produced between them, the correspondence between
Goethe and Kestner continued to the
end of the century. Lotte saw Goethe
in Weimar in 1816, when she was sixty-
three years old ; she was still beautiful,
but her head shook with palsy. She
died in 1828. The second part of *Wer-*
ther represents the agony of a jealous husband. This was inspired by Brentano,
an Italian merchant resident in Leipsic,
a widower with five children, who had
married Maximiliane, the daughter of

Sophie la Roche. Goethe loved her as an elder brother, but her husband scarcely approved of the intimacy. Merck tells us that Brentano's ideas went very little beyond his business, and that it was dispiriting for Goethe to have to look for his young girl friend among barrels of herrings and piles of cheeses. "Goethe," he says, "much consoles her for the smell of oil and cheese, and for her husband's manners."

Götz and *Werther* formed the solid foundation of Goethe's fame. They were read from one end of Germany to the other. It is difficult to imagine that the same man can have produced both works, so different are they in matter and in style. *Werther* represents the languid sentimentalism, the passionate despair, which possessed an age vexed by evils which nothing but the knife can cure, and tortured by the presence of a high ideal which revealed to it at once

the depth of its misery and the hopeless-
ness of a better lot. *Götz* was the first
manly appeal to the chivalry of German
spirit, which, caught up by other voices,
sounded throughout the fatherland like
the call of a warder's trumpet, till it produced a national courage founded on the
recollection of an illustrious past, which
overthrew the might of the conqueror at
the moment when he seemed about to
dominate the world. *Werther* is the echo
of Rousseau, the lamentation of a suffering humanity; *Götz* is the prototype of
Stein, the corner stone of a renovated
Empire. *Götz*, in its short, sharp dialogue, recalls the pregnant terseness of
mediæval German, before it was spoilt
by the imitators of Ciceronian Latinity.
Werther, as soft and melodious as Plato,
was the first revelation to the world of
that marvellous style which, in the hands
of a master, compels a language which
is as rich as Greek to be also as musical.

These two great works were not the Satires. only occupations of Goethe at this time. In Wetzlar he had translated Goldsmith's *Deserted Village*, and had written a number of small poems addressed to Lotte. The spring of 1773, which witnessed the publication of *Götz*, saw him actively employed as an advocate. His relations with his father became easier. His literary success brought him a number of friends,—the young Counts Stolberg, and Von Schönborn, a friend of Klopstock's. He also began to correspond with Lavater the physiognomist, and with Klopstock himself. To the latter half of this year are to be referred a number of satirical poems, aimed at prevailing follies of the time, clever and amusing, but of little permanent value. In *Peter Brey* he satirized the meddler Leuchsenring, who, with soft tread and lamblike manners, interfered with the family rela-

tions of Herder. *Satyros* is directed
against the prophets of the school of
Nature, who bid us return to Nature
without remembering how coarse and
repellent some aspects of Nature are.
Bahrdt had translated the Bible into
modern cultivated German; Goethe
wrote a prologue to this newest of divine
revelations, in which the four evangelists
appear each with his attendant animal.
Of yet another kind is the *Fair of
Plundersweilern*, in which the hucksters
and booth-keepers represent the motley
variety of human life and the character-
istics of modern littérateurs. It is a
foretaste of the second part of *Faust*.
Harlequin's Marriage is only preserved
in fragments ; it was perhaps too coarse
and personal to be published. The most
important of these writings is *Gods,
Heroes, and Wieland,* a dialogue in the
style of Lucian written at a sitting over
a bottle of Burgundy, in which Alcestis,

Mercury, Hercules, Euripides, and other
ancient worthies appear to Wieland in
all their original greatness, and upbraid
him with the mean and paltry representation of them which he had given to the
world. Wieland was the apostle of an
emasculated antiquity. Goethe would
make the gods speak in their own large
utterance if they spoke at all. Wieland
revenged himself by recommending the
satire in his paper, the *Deutsche Merkur*, as a delicate piece of persiflage
worthy of the study of his readers. In
November Goethe's sister Cornelia was
married to Schlosser and left Strasburg.
Goethe felt the loss deeply. She lived
but a short time. Her married life was
tortured with perpetual suffering, and
she died in 1777.

The beginning of 1774 is marked by
a new passion and a new work. Cres-
pel had invented a plan for enlivening
their social meetings ; each man was to

draw lots for a partner, and for the time
to consider her as his wife.   Three
times Goethe drew the name of Anna
Sibylla Münch, a pleasant girl of sixteen,
daughter of a merchant.   One of the
favourite topics of the day was the trial
of Beaumarchais, which ended on February 16th, 1774.   Immediately afterwards his *Mémoires* or pleadings were
published, and from the fourth of these
Clavigo. the play of *Clavigo* was arranged.   It
represents a young writer of ambition
deserting the woman to whom he is
engaged and breaking her heart.   The
fifth act, in which Clavigo kills himself, is Goethe's own creation.   The real
Clavigo died, a distinguished man of letters, in 1806.   The piece was written in
eight days, and published on June 1st.
It had a great success, and still keeps
the stage.   But Goethe's best friends
were disappointed with it.   Merck told
him not to write such trash, as others

could do that as well. In reality there
is no period of Goethe's life in which his
literary activity was so prodigious, or
when he was more fully occupied with
literary plans which had reference to
the deepest problems of human nature.
To this time belong the conceptions of
Cæsar, Faust, Mahomet, the *Wandering
Jew,* and *Prometheus.* The first was
soon given up ; of the second, the first
monologue, the dialogue between Faust
and Mephistopheles, and part of the
scenes with Gretchen, were now written.
He has told us in his *Autobiography*
what he intended to make of *Mahomet.*
In five acts he was to show us how the
purity of prophetic zeal is recognised
by love, rejected by envy, sullied by
human weakness, spiritualized by death.
To write this drama he had studied the
Koran through and through ; only a few
fragments were completed. Of the
Wandering Jew very little remains to

us. The design, conceived in Italy, of making a great work on the subject was never carried out. The *Prometheus* was completed in two acts. The monologue of *Prometheus*, included in the *Lyrical Poems*, was written at the same time; but it is doubtful whether it was intended to form part of the drama. These works are to be referred to the study of the ethics of Spinoza, for whom Goethe now began to feel a deep reverence, which continued throughout his life. The calm repose of Spinoza's mind spread over his own like a breath of peace; his systematic and well-ordered reasoning was the best antidote to Goethe's passionate waywardness. Goethe now acquired a wider view of all the relations of the moral and natural world; he felt that he had never seen the universe so clearly. The time spent at Frankfort was also largely occupied with Art. His room was covered with the works of his pencil,

and a number of poems on the subject
of the artist's life arose from the same
influence.

The summer of 1774 was spent in a
journey to the Rhine.   On July 12th
Basedow, the educational reformer, came
to Frankfort; three days afterwards
Goethe went with him to Ems, where
he found Lavater, who had been with
him in the previous month.   The three
went down the Lahn together, and
reached Coblentz on July 18th.   Here
the famous dinner took place at which
Lavater explained the secrets of the
Apocalypse to a clergyman, Basedow
demonstrated the uselessness of baptism
to a dancing-master, while Goethe, the
worldling between the two prophets,
made the best of his time with the fish
and the chicken.   They then went down
the Rhine to Elberfeld, where Goethe
found his old Strasburg friend Jung-
Stilling, and back to Pempelfort, near

*Rhine
journey.*

Düsseldorf, the house of Fritz Jacobi,
where Goethe also met Jacobi's wife
Betty, his sister Charlotte, his aunt
Johanna Fahlmer, and his friend W.
Heinse.   Their letters are full of the
effect which he produced upon them.
Heinse says—" I know of no man in the
whole history of learning who, at such
an age, was so completely full of original
genius."   Jacobi writes—" Goethe is the
man whom my heart required ; my
character will now gain its proper sta-
bility ; the man is complete from head to
foot."   Again he says, that you could not
be an hour with him, without seeing that
it would be ridiculous to suppose that
he could think or act otherwise than he
really thinks and acts.   No change could
make him fairer or better ; his nature
has followed its own development, as the
growth of a seed, or of a flower on a tree.
Nor were these impressions evanescent.
Forty years afterwards he writes of

these times—" What hours! what days!
I seemed to have a new soul. From
that moment forth I was determined
that I would never leave you."

Goethe returned to Frankfort at the Frankfort.
beginning of August. The autumn
brought new friends, drawn to him by
the fame of the newly published *Werther*. Among these was Klopstock,
twenty-five years older than Goethe, the
author of the *Messiah*, the acknowledged
head of German poets. On December
11 Goethe was surprised by the visit
of a stranger, whom he at first took for
Fr. Jacobi. It was Karl Ludwig von
Knebel, who was travelling with the
two young princes of Saxe-Weimar, the
reigning duke Karl August, then just
seventeen, and his younger brother Constantine. They were on their way to
France with their tutor, Count Görz, and
they could not pass through Frankfort
without making the acquaintance of the

E

new genius who had risen upon their
country.   Goethe went to see them, was
warnily received, and talked with them
about the condition and prospects of
Germany.   This meeting decided the
future course of Goethe's life.   Knebel
thought Goethe "the best of men, the
most lovable of mankind."   The princes
invited him to visit them at Mainz,
where they would stay longer than at
Frankfort.   The visit lasted from December 13 to 15, when they went on
to Carlsruhe, where the duke was to
meet his intended bride.   Goethe took
the opportunity of reconciling himself
with Wieland, who lived in Weimar.
On his return he found Fräulein von
Klettenberg dead.   " My Klettenberg is
dead," he writes, " before I had an idea
that she was dangerously ill.   Dead and
buried in my absence !   She who was so
dear, so much to me."   Frederike was lost
to him, Charlotte, Maximiliane, and his

sister were married. Some attachment was a necessity of his nature. He now came under the influence of Lili Schöne- Lili. mann, the daughter of a rich banker, whose father was dead, but whose mother conducted the business, and held one of the most brilliant salons in Frankfort. This passion seemed to be of a more lasting nature than the others. Goethe was drawn into the whirl of society. He is described as moving in brilliantly-lighted rooms, in a gold-laced coat, passing from party to concert, from concert to ball, held captive by a fairhaired girl with a pair of bright eyes. Such was Goethe in the carnival time. To Lili's influence we owe several of his smaller poems, *Neue Liebe neues Leben*, *Herz mein Herz was soll das geben*, *Heidenröslein*, and two little vaudevilles, *Erwin und Elmire* and *Claudine von Villa Bella*. The first contains some pretty songs, notably *Das Veilchen*, set

to music by Mozart.   The play is founded
on the ballad of " Edwin and Angelina "
in the *Vicar of Wakefield.*   The latter
half belongs to an earlier period, and is
complete in itself.   *Claudine von Villa
Bella* has one good character, the pro-
digal son Crugantino ; the ballad which
is sung at the crisis of the plot was
written during the Rhine journey with
Jacobi.   To this period also belongs
Stella. *Stella*, a comedy for lovers, a strange,
wild play, full of extravagant passion.
The weak-minded hero Fernando
marries two wives one after the other.
They meet together in an inn, and he
is reduced to extremity of misery.   He
loves them both, and they both love him.
Finally, the first wife, Stella, surrenders
her rights, and they agree all to live together.   The play in this form suggested
to Canning the parody of the *Rovers ;
or, the Double Arrangement.*   In 1806
Goethe altered the close by making

Fernando shoot himself and Stella take poison. It is seldom performed; but Stella is a fine character for a great actress. It is said to be founded on an occurrence in the Jacobi family.

Neither family approved of the engagement between the youthful couple. Goethe's parents thought Lili too much of a fine lady; they had a suspicion, which was well founded, that her wealth had no very sure foundation. Frau Schönemann did not think that Goethe, with all his genius, would make a good husband for her child. Cornelia Schlosser was strongly opposed to the match. Goethe tore himself away, and went for a tour in Switzerland. His companions were the brothers Stolberg, noisy, wild young noblemen, who in May had stayed at Goethe's house. They gave Goethe's mother the name of Frau Aya, which she ever afterwards retained. On his journey Goethe visited the duke of Saxe-

Swiss journey.

Weimar and his betrothed at Carlsruhe,
his sister at Emmendingen, and Lavater
at Zurich. He bore with him the constant
memory of Lili; he wore a golden heart
which she had given him round his neck.
He climbed the St Gotthard on her
birthday, and looked with longing eyes
to the promised land of Italy. But a
stronger power drew him home again,
and he returned. At Strasburg he met
his old friends, and saw Zimmermann,
the writer on solitude. He showed
Goethe a profile portrait of Frau von
Stein, who lived at Weimar, with which
he was enchanted.

Return.   He returned to Frankfort on July 20.
August was spent delightfully with Lili
at Offenbach; his letters speak of nothing but her. September and the fair-
time at Frankfort brought back his
troubles. His position is described in
the poem *Lili's Park*. He is the half-
tamed bear who is held by magic bands

amongst the birds and the fish, and yet sees a door left a little open for escape, and swears that he has the power to pass it. During this last period of his passion he translated part of the Song of Solomon. He wrote some scenes in *Faust*—the walk in the garden, the first conversation with Mephistopheles, the interview with the scholar, the scene in Auerbach's cellar. *Egmont* was also begun under the stimulus of the American Rebellion. A way of escaping from his embarrassments was unexpectedly opened to him. The duke of Weimar passed through Frankfort both before and after his marriage, which took place on October 3. He invited Goethe to stay at Weimar, and it was arranged that one of the duke's household, who was expected every day with a new carriage, should bring the new guest with him. He took leave of every one, including Lili. But the carriage did not come ; a second leave-taking was impossible. He remained all day in the house working at *Egmont*, going out only at night. Once he stood by Lili's window, heard her sing his songs, and saw her shadow on the curtain. He could not linger longer in the town. He started for Heidelberg, hoping to meet the carriage, determined if it did not come to go on to Italy. He was summoned hastily back by a messenger, found the carriage at Frankfort, and entered Weimar in the early morning of November 7, 1775. It was not for his happiness or for Lili's that they should have married. She afterwards thanked him deeply for the firmness with which he overcame a temptation to which she would have yielded.

Weimar. At this time the smaller German courts were beginning to take an interest in German literature. Before the Seven Years' War the whole of German culture had been French. Even now, German

writers found but scant acceptance at
Berlin or Vienna. The princes of the
smaller States, shut out from the great
world of politics, surrounded themselves
with literature and Art, and with men
who would be likely to give an interest
to their lives. The duke of Brunswick
had made Lessing his librarian at Wol-
fenbüttel, and had not objected to the
publication of *Emilia Galotti.* Emerich
Joseph, the worldly elector and arch-
bishop of Mainz, was devoted to Munich
and the theatre, and made his stage one
of the best in Europe. The margrave
of Baden had invited Klopstock to his
court, and delighted to associate with
himself the author of the *Messiah*, the
" poet of religion and of his country."
The duke of Würtemberg paid special
attention to education ; he promoted the
views of Schubart, and founded the
school in which Schiller was educated.
Hanover offered a home to Zimmer-

mann, and encouraged the development
of Schlegel. Darmstadt was specially
fortunate. Caroline, the wife of the
landgrave, had surrounded herself with
a literary circle, of which Merck was the
moving spirit. She had collected and
privately printed the odes of Klopstock ;
and her death, in 1774, seemed to leave
Darmstadt a desert. Her daughter
Louise, the youngest of eight children,
seemed to have inherited something of
her mother's qualities, veiled by a serious
and retiring temper. She married, on
October 3, 1775, the young duke of Weimar, who had just attained his majority.
She reigned over that illustrious court
respected and admired, but repelled
rather than attracted by its brilliancy
and eccentricity. The place which she
would naturally have occupied was taken
by the duchess Amalia, mother of the
grand-duke. She was of the house of
Brunswick, and after two years of mar-

riage had been left a widow at nineteen
with two sons. She committed their
education to Count Görz, a prominent
character in the history of the time.
She afterwards summoned Wieland to
instruct the elder, and Knebel to teach
the younger. The *Deutsche Merkur*,
founded in 1773 to diminish the influence
of the school of Klopstock, gave Weimar
importance in the literary world. The
duchess was a great lover of the stage ;
and the best play-writers of Germany
worked for Weimar. The palace and
the theatre were burnt down in 1774,
and the duchess had to content herself
with amateurs. After her son's marriage
she lived in the simple country houses
which surround the capital, the lofty
Ettersburg, the low-lying Tiefurt, the
far-seeing height of Belvedere. Each
of these was awakened to new life by
the genius of Goethe. The duke, eigh-
teen years of age, was simple in his

tastes, a hater of etiquette and con-
straint, true, honest, and steadfast, fond
of novelty and excitement, of great courage and activity ; his impulses, rarely
checked, led him rather to chivalrous
enterprise than to undesirable excess.
His brother, Prince Constantine, had
perhaps more talent but less character
than the grand-duke.   He took but little
part in the Weimar life, and died in
1793.

Goethe in
Weimar.
Upon this society Goethe, in the
strength and beauty of youth, rose like
a star.   From the moment of his arrival
he became the inseparable and indispensable companion of the grand-duke.   He
subdued the affections of all he met with.
Wieland said that his soul was as full of
him as a dewdrop of the morning sun.
He was, he said, take him all in all, the
greatest, best, most noble human being
that God had ever created.   The first
months at Weimar were spent in a wild

round of pleasure. Goethe was treated
as a guest. In the autumn, journeys,
rides, shooting parties ; in the winter,
balls, masquerades, skating parties by
torchlight, dancing at peasants' feasts,
filled up their time. Evil reports flew
about Germany ; the court of Weimar
had a bad name ; Klopstock wrote letters
of solemn advice, and forbade his young
friend Stolberg to accept an appoint-
ment which the duke had offered to him.
We do not know, and we need not examine, how much of these reports was
true. Goethe wrote to Klopstock that
if Stolberg came he would find them no
worse, and perhaps even better, than he
had known them before. We may believe that no decencies were disregarded
except the artificial restrictions of courtly
etiquette. Goethe and the duke dined
together and bathed together ; the duke
addressed his friend by the familiar *thou*.
Goethe slept in his chamber, and tended

him when he was ill. In the spring
Goethe had to decide whether he would
go or stay. In April the duke gave him
the little garden-house by the side of the
Ilm, with its lofty roof, in which he lived
for the next eight years. In June he
invested him with the title, a matter so
important in German eyes, of Geheim-
legationsrath, with a seat and voice in
the privy council, and an income of £180
a year. By accepting this position he
was bound to Weimar for ever. We
may here mention the different grades of
service through which Goethe passed.
In January, 1779, he undertook the commission of war ; on September 5, 1779,
he became Geheim-rath; in September,
1781, he received an addition to his
salary of £30. This was afterwards
raised by £60 more, and in 1816 he
received £450, with an additional allow-
ance for the expense of a carriage. In
April, 1782, he was ennobled by the

emperor, and took for his arms a silver star in an azure field; in June of the same year he became president of the chamber *ad interim.* We know that Goethe devoted himself with industry and enthusiasm to the public business ; he made himself acquainted with every part of his master's territory; he did his best to develop its resources ; he opened mines and disseminated education ; he threw himself with vigour into the reconstruction of the tiny army. A complete account of his labours in this field cannot be known until the secrets of the Goethe house at Weimar are fully revealed to the curious. We shall then perhaps find that Goethe cannot be fairly charged with want of patriotism, or coldness to the national interest, and that his apparent indifference to the rising of 1813 must be considered in connexion with his resistance to the encroachments of Austria at an earlier time.

Goethe's life was at no time complete
without the influence of a noble-hearted
woman. This he now found in Charlotte von Stein, a lady of the court, wife
of the master of the horse. She was
thirty-three years of age, mother of seven
children. His letters to her extend over
a period of fifty years. Until his journey
to Italy he made her acquainted with
every action, every thought of his mind,
all the working of his brain. He calls
her by every endearing epithet — the
sweet entertainment of his inmost heart,
the dear unconquerable source of his
happiness, the sweet dream of his life,
the anodyne of his sorrows, his happiness, his gold, his magnet, whom he
loves in presence and absence, sleeping
and waking, from whom he can never
bear to be parted. Many of Goethe's
writings were from this time inspired by
the necessities of the court. One group
of them is formed by the succession of

masks or ballets which were performed
to celebrate the birthday of the grand-
duchess Louise. *The Four Seasons,
The Procession of Laplanders, the Nine
Female Virtues, The Dance of the
Planets,* are sufficiently explained by
their names. Others were called for by
the amateur theatre, which now was
forced to supply the place of the regular
drama. The stage was often set in the
open air, the seats cut out of turf ; the
side scenes, of trimmed box, still exist
at Belvedere and Ettersburg. The
actors were the duchess-mother and her
sons, the civil servants and the officers,
the ladies in waiting and the pages.
Goethe was very good in comic parts ;
in solemn tragedy, as in his own *Orestes,*
he could best interpret the dignity of the
ancient stage. Musæus, head-master of
the public school, was set to play low
comedy ; Knebel represented the digni-
fied hero. The chief professional sup-

F

port of the stage was Corona Schröter, whom the duke and Goethe personally carried off from Leipsic. On this visit he saw, after a long absence, Catherine Schönkopf, Oeser, and other friends of his youth. Goethe represented most of his earlier pieces on the Weimar stage. He wrote nothing of great importance for it till the first sketch of his *Iphigenie.* But several smaller pieces owe their origin to this cause. *Proserpina* is a melodrama ; *Die Geschwister,* though it plays but half an hour, is a psychological study of rare delicacy and interest ; *Jery und Bätely* and *Die Fischerin* are little operas composed to suit the Weimar taste. *Scherz, List, und Rache* is an imitation of the Italian style.

Journeys. Besides numerous visits to the court of the Thuringian princes, sojournings at Dornberg and at Ilmenau, that retired nook of the Weimar fatherland which still attracts many a pilgrim lover of

Goethe, the first ten years at Weimar
were interrupted by longer journeys.
One of these was the winter Harz
journey in December, 1777, undertaken
suddenly to make the acquaintance of
Plessing, a self-torturing hypochondriac,
who had written to the poet for advice.
With Goethe's help Plessing recovered
from his melancholy, visited him at
Weimar, and entertained him, as professor at Duisburg, on his return from
the campaign in France. A visit to
Dessau inspired the improvements of
the park and grounds at Weimar, which
now make it so attractive. The close
of 1779 was occupied by a winter
journey to Switzerland, undertaken with
the duke and a small retinue. Two
days were spent at Frankfort with
Goethe's parents. Sesenheim was
visited, and left with satisfaction and
contentment. At Strasburg the travellers found Lili happily married, with a

new-born child.   At Emmendingen
Goethe stood by his sister's grave, and
saw her successor, Johanna Fahlmer,
Jacobi's aunt.   The Swiss journey began
at Basel.   The chief object of it was
to forward the health and education of
the young duke.   It was a bold plan
to execute in October and November.
From Bern they made the tour of the
Bernese Oberland.   From Geneva, by
the advice of De Saussure, they visited
Mont Blanc and the valley of Chamouni ;
they crossed the Furka, not without
danger, in the middle of November,
descended the St Gotthard to Lucerne,
and visited Lavater at Zurich, the goal
and summit of their tour.   From this
time Lavater lost his influence over
Goethe ; and in 1786 the poet would
gladly have run away from Weimar to
avoid him.   In December the friends
went by the lake of Constance and the
falls of the Rhine to Stuttgart, where,

on December 14, Goethe saw Schiller
for the first time. He was a student at
the Academy, and in Goethe's presence
received the prize.

The return to Weimar, on January
13, was the beginning of a new era.
The period of genius and eccentricity
was at an end ; that of order and regularity succeeded. As an outward sign
of the change, the duke cut off his pig-
tail, an example which was long without
imitators. Wieland said that the Swiss
winter journey was the greatest of
Goethe's dramas. In the same serious
mood Goethe began to write history.
He chose for his subject Duke Bern-
hard of Saxe-Weimar, the knight-errant
of the Reformation. He spent much
time and trouble in collecting materials,
but at length reasonably concluded that
his strength lay elsewhere. At this
time also he began to write *Tasso*, and
adapted the *Birds* of Aristophanes to

modern circumstances. His deeper
thoughts were concentrated in *Wilhelm
Meister*. Countess Werther, the sister
of the great minister Baron von Stein,
whom he visited at Neunheiligen, was
transferred in living portraiture to its
pages. His efforts for the development
of the duke's dominion naturally led him
to the study of science. The opening
and direction of mines induced him to
study geology; the classification of early
forms of life led him to osteology and
anatomy. Goethe was always fond of
children. The young Herders and
Wielands spent much time in his garden, sometimes digging for Easter eggs
which had been carefully concealed. In
the spring of 1783 Fritz, the son of
Charlotte von Stein, then ten years old,
came to live with him in his garden
house. In the autumn they took a
journey together in the Harz. At
Ilmenau was written the touching poem

of that name on the duke's birthday.
Goethe reviews in it their common
friendship and activity as far as it has
yet gone, and a few days afterwards, as
he slept in the hut on the Gickelhahn,
he wrote in pencil the world-known lines
in which he anticipates for himself that
rest and silence which then held en-
chained the summits of the hills and the
birds of the wood. In the following
year another journey was undertaken in
the Harz for the study of mineralogy.
But this was only a relaxation from more
serious affairs. In 1785 the Fürsten-
bund or league of princes was formed,
under the supremacy of Frederick the
Great, to resist the ambition of Austria
under Joseph II. The duke of Saxe-
Weimar took an important part in form-
ing this league, and in the negotiations
which preceded it. Goethe was his indispensable adviser, and must on this
occasion, if not on others, have taken a

keen interest in politics and in the independence of Germany.

**Leaves
Weimar.**   The year 1786 marks an epoch in
Goethe's life.   He had now been ten
years in Weimar, and he must have felt
that his own inward development, and
the work which he was most fitted to
do in the world, were not advancing
as favourably as they should.   He had
written little of first-rate importance.
His *Lyrics* were of intense beauty and
of deep meaning, but they were short
and fugitive.   He had brought with him
from Frankfort the sketches of *Faust*
and *Egmont*, but little had been done to
them since.   His occasional writings for
the amateur theatre, or for court festivi-
ties, were not such as to add to his solid
reputation in Germany.   *Iphigenie* was
the one great work of poetry which belongs entirely to this period ; but that
had not received its final form.   *Tasso*
was conceived ; but only two acts were

written, and these in prose. *Wilhelm Meister* is the most exact expression of this portion of Goethe's life ; but loftily as it now towers above the level of his smaller dramas, it did not then satisfy the author, nor was it in a state to be published. For the completion of these works Goethe required leisure and repose, impossible to obtain in the distraction and pleasures of a court. This became more apparent to him as he set himself to collect his scattered writings. Four volumes were soon completed; but the preparation of the other four convinced him how much labour many of his poems still required for perfection. Another cause of discontent was his relation to Frau von Stein. It could not have been more intimate. She was all to Goethe, and more than Gretchen, Frederike, Lili, or his sister Cornelia had been. He communicated to her every thought and every action of his

life. The relation was pardonable ; to a
character like Goethe's it was natural ;
but it became every year more difficult
and more full of danger. The ardent
devotion which sat well on the im-
petuosity of youth was less becoming
and less possible to the man of middle
age. Yet the tie could not be severed
without a struggle, and the wrench could
not be effected without an enforced
absence. To these necessities, the need
of quiet for composition, and for deliber-
ately rearranging the circumstances of
his life, was added the stress of other
impulses. Goethe had all his life been
fascinated by the practice of Art. Indeed
it was not until he had discovered at
Rome the limitation of his powers, that
he definitely renounced the hope of becoming an artist. He tried almost every
branch in turn. He drew in pencil and
in sepia, sketched, painted in oil, en-
graved on copper and wood, and etched.

For these occupations he had but little leisure; at this time he attributed his slow improvement rather to want of labour than to want of power. He saw infinite possibilities of advance in a life of freedom spent under the inspiration of sunny skies, and amidst the environment of the highest art.

Of still deeper interest and importance Science. were his scientific researches. In these he aspired to detect the secrets of nature; he succeeded in seeing, as in a vision, the great scheme of evolution applied to all phenomena of the natural and moral world, which the labours of many workers have revealed to us in our own day. He longed for time and leisure to perfect these ideas, to base them on solid fact. Goethe has not added much of positive value to the treasury of scientific truth, but he deserves the credit of having discerned the right method of inquiry when it was

obscure to many, and of having thrown
that glow of imagination over dry and
technical inquiry, without which no great
discoveries can be made. His inquiries
into the nature of light belong to a later
time. He began with physiognomy under the auspices of Lavater. From this
he was led to the study of anatomy, and
especially to the comparison of the
skeletons of men and animals. In this
department he made a real discovery,
that the intermaxillary bone which exists
in the lower animals is found in the
human subject in a rudimentary state,—
that it is seen distinctly in youth, but, as
years advance, is united with the body of
the skull. The discovery that the skull
itself is only a development of the verte-
bræ of the spine was made a little later.
Goethe was led to this further step by
picking up the head of a sheep on the
shore of the Lido at Venice. The care of
his garden-cottage naturally led him to

the study of plants. He soon found himself attracted to wide and comprehensive
generalizations. The *Metamorphoses of
Plants* was not published till 1790, but
the idea which had possession of his
mind was a solid contribution to the
science of botany. Goethe sought to
discover an original or standard flower,
from which, as from a Platonic ideal
type, all existing flowers were deflexions
and aberrations. In this he followed an
unscientific method ; but he clearly saw
that all the different parts of the plant,
except the stem and the root, might be
regarded as modifications of the leaf ;
that leaf, calyx, corolla, bud, pistil, and
stamen were all referable to the same
type ; and that whether a plant produced
leaves, or flowers, or fruit, depended on
the differentiation of the nutrition which
it received. Less fortunate were his
speculations in geology, to which he
devoted a very large portion of his time

and thoughts.   It is something that he
recognised the importance and reality of
that science, then in its infancy, which
has had to undergo more than its due
share of obloquy and distrust.   But he
was of necessity a follower of Werner,
who based his classification of rocks
rather on the minerals which they contained than upon an examination of the
fossil remains of organic life.   All these
causes contributed together to one end.
His desire to complete the great poetical
works which he had begun, to disen-
tangle his life from the complexities
which had entwined themselves round
it, to give a fair trial to his impulses
towards Art, to afford opportunity for the
careful and systematic interrogation of
Nature, and. above all, a longing to
possess his soul in peace, and solemnly
to probe in silence the depths of his own
being, conspired together to drive him
from Weimar to the land which he had

yearned after from boyhood. The reso-
lution, slowly formed, was boldly exe-
cuted. In the summer of 1785 he had
visited Carlsbad for the first time, passed
a pleasant month in the company of the
duchess Louise, Herder, and Frau von
Stein. In July, 1786, he paid it a second
visit. After five weeks of brilliant
society, very favourable to his health,
spent in revising his works for the press,
he stole secretly away. The duke alone
knew that he designed an absence of
some duration. In the strictest incognito, in the guise of a German merchant,
he drove alone to the land of the citron
and the orange.

Goethe's Italian journey, the most Italy.
momentous epoch in the development of
his intellectual life, lasted from September 3, 1786, to June 18, 1788. Assum-
ing the common German name of
Müller, he journeyed in the strictest
incognito by way of Munich, where he

studied the picture gallery and the
collection of antiquities ; by the Lake of
Garda, where he began his metrical
version of the *Iphigenie* ; by Verona,
where he saw the first specimen of
Roman building in Italy in the stupend-
ous amphitheatre ; by Vicenza, where
he was attracted by the grace and harmony of the classical Palladio ; by
Padua, where he neglected the frescos
of Giotto, but rose to a clear conception
of the form of the *original plant* by the
marks on the leaves of a palm in the
botanical garden ; to Venice, where for
the first time he was able to taste the
charm and richness of southern life. As
he proceeded farther, Ferrara spoke to
him of Tasso ; Bologna showed him the
great masters of the academic school,
who have now grown pale and dim before the predecessors of Raphael ; Flor-
ence interested him a little ; Assisi drew
his attention, not to the triple church of

Saint Francis, that unrivalled museum
of religious Art, but to the little ruined
temple which no modern traveller would
notice but for the name of Goethe;
Spoleto again delighted him with the
remains of ancient architecture. He
reached Rome on October 28. His first Rome.
stay lasted till February. The constant
companion of his studies was the painter
Tischbein, who helped him to disen-
tangle the many difficulties of the old
Rome and the new. He lived chiefly
among the German artists and men of
letters who frequented the Caffé Greco.
Among these were Angelica Kaufmann
and Moritz, known for his travels
in England, who deepened Goethe's
knowledge of German versification, and
prepared him for the composition of
Iphigenia. Although Goethe occupied
himself chiefly with drawing, he was
able to announce on June 6 that this
work was finished. The second *Iphi-*

G

génie, written in verse, was the first
important fruit of the Italian journey.
It is in very strong contrast with *Götz
von Berlichingen*. It is written in the
strictest classical form. Although based
on the *Iphigenia in Tauris* of Euripides,
it has little in common with it. In Euripides Thoas is represented as a cruel
barbarian, against whom it is justifiable
to employ every artifice of fraud or
violence. In Goethe the characters are
ennobled by a higher principle ; and the
struggle between truth and falsehood is
made a prominent motive of the piece.
When Thoas discovers that, according
to the oracle of Apollo, the return of
Orestes' sister to Greece will satisfy the
anger of the gods, he gives his consent,
and his last words are a friendly farewell.
Towards the end of February Goethe
left Rome for Naples. Here he was attracted less by the remains of antiquity,
even the new revelations of Herculaneum

and Pompeii, than by the prospects of
Nature, the bay, the islands, the volcano,
the thousand beauties which make the
gulf unrivalled in the world, and by the
multitudinous and teeming life which
throngs the endless quays that line the
shore. Sorrento stimulated him to the *Tasso.*
revisal of *Torquato Tasso*, but he did not
complete the drama till his return from
Italy. It did not appear in print till the
spring of 1790. The play had a special
fascination for him as a picture of his
own distracted life. He could depict
with feeling the struggle between the
actual and the ideal, the ill-assorted
connexion of a passionate poet with the
jealous and artificial environment of a
court. At the end of March Goethe Sicily.
sailed to Sicily; rolled up in his cloak,
he meditated the composition of his
Tasso. Sicily struck him, as it must
strike all travellers who have studied
the ancient world, as a revelation of

Greece. It is, if one may say so, more Greek than Greece itself. Its mountains, streams, trees, flowers, the form of its boats and its pottery, the habits of the people, the quivering smile of the bright blue sea fringed with golden sand, represent completely the Greece of the *Odyssey* and of the choruses of Euripides. Goethe was overmastered by this powerful influence. He sketched and began *Nausicaa*, the story of the *Odyssey* in dramatic form, which always remained a fragment. He returned to Rome in June. The rest of the year was spent in the city and its neighbourhood, in the serious study of drawing, for which unfortunately he had but little talent, and in the composition *Egmont.* of *Egmont*, a work begun with the approval of his father in the early Frankfort days. It was finished in September, 1787, and appeared in the Easter of the following year. Although *Egmont*

still keeps the stage, it has grave faults.
It is an unfortunate mixture of the
natural and ideal treatment. The licence
with which the scenes are transposed in
modern performance shows how much
the work lacks symmetry and cohesion.
Schiller criticized it severely, as being
untrue to history. He described the
close, where all difficulties are solved by
the appearance of Clärchen, as a *deus
ex machinâ*, or a *salto mortale* into the
world of opera. The music of Beethoven has contributed to it a charm of
art which was necessary to its com-
pleteness. Besides this, Goethe re-wrote
for publication his early vaudevilles of
Erwin und Elmire and *Claudine von
Villa Bella.* The carnival of 1788 was
of importance to his experience. He
wrote some scenes of *Faust:* the scene *Faust.*
in the witches' kitchen was composed in
the Borghese gardens. At the end of
April he took a sad farewell of Italy,

and arrived at Weimar in the middle of June.

Return to Weimar. From this time his life takes a new colour. He had learned in Italy not only new principles of Art,—not only that a work of Art, whatever of Gothic ornament it may possess, must be solid, firm, and simple in its construction as a Grecian temple,—but he had also learned that life itself should be a work of Art. He was determined henceforth to be himself, to break the bonds which had confined him and the distractions which had confused him, to possess his soul sacred and inviolable for the purposes of his life. He was relieved of the presidency of the chamber and of the war commission, but in a manner which did him the greatest honour. His relations with Frau von Stein, which had been one reason of his leaving Weimar, began to cool. One of their last friendly meetings was in a journey to Rudolstadt

where Goethe met Schiller. Neither
knew the influence which the other
would have upon his life. Their relations were those of shyness, and partly
even of dislike. Goethe's friendship
with Frau von Stein was to receive a
final blow. In the autumn of 1788, Christiane Vulpius.
walking aimlessly through the park, he
met Christiane Vulpius, a young girl
who presented him with a petition in
favour of her brother. She had golden
curling locks, round cheeks, laughing
eyes, a neatly rounded figure; she
looked, as has been said, " like a young
Dionysus." Goethe took her into his
house, and she became his wife in con-
science, and the mother of his children.
He did not marry her till 1806, when
the terrors of the French occupation
made him anxious for the position of his
eldest son. It is true she had but little
education, and that he could not take her
into society ; but she made him a good

and loving wife, and her quick mother-
wit made her available as an intellectual
companion.   To these days of early
married life belong the Roman elegies,
which, although Italian and pagan in
form, colour, and sensuality, were written in Germany from home experiences.

Cam-   We must pass rapidly over the next
paigns   six years, until Goethe's genius received
a new impulse and direction by his
friendship with Schiller.   In the spring
of 1790 he travelled to Venice, to meet
the duchess Amalia.   The Venetian
epigrams, still more outspoken in sensuality than the Roman, were the fruit
of this journey.   In the autumn of the
same year he accompanied the duke to
Silesia, the first of those military journeys which strike so discordant a note
in the harmonious tenor of his existence.
The year 1791 offered a quiet contrast
to the movement of the year before.
He began to take a more special interest

in the University at Jena, in which his young friend Fritz von Stein had now entered as a student, and his time was more and more occupied with the study of colours, the least happy and successful of his scientific labours. In the autumn of 1791 Goethe was able to devote himself regularly to a task which had informally occupied his first years in Weimar. The new theatre was completed, and Goethe was made director of it. It was in this capacity that he was best known to the citizens of Weimar. He had the final decision on every detail of piece, scenery, and acting ; in later years his seat was in a large arm-chair in the middle of the pit, and applause was scarcely permitted until he gave the signal for it. The German stage owes perhaps as much to Goethe as to Lessing. The *répertoire* of the Weimar theatre was stocked with pieces of solid merit which long

held their place. Shakespeare was
seriously performed, and the actors were
instructed in the delivery of blank verse.
Stress was laid on the excellence of the
ensemble as against the predominance of
particular stars. The theatre was considered as a school not only of elevat-
ing amusement but of national culture.
Goethe wrote the *Gross Cophta* for the
Weimar stage, a piece founded on the
history of Cagliostro and the diamond
necklace. He was fascinated by the
story as a foreboding of the coming
horrors of the Revolution. In these
events he was destined to take a more
active part than he expected. In
August, 1792, he accompanied the duke
to the campaign in the Ardennes.
Passing by Frankfort, where he visited
his mother, he joined the allied armies
at Longwy. He beguiled the tedious
siege of Verdun by writing an account
of his theory of colours in a leaky tent;

and on the disastrous day of Valmy,
which he recognised as the birth of a
new era, he sought the thickest of the
fight that he might experience the
dangerous rapture of the cannon-fever.
He retreated with the Prussian army,
spent five weeks with his friend Jacobi
at Pempelfort, and on his return to
Weimar at the end of the year found
that the duke had built him a spacious
house in the square now called the
Goethe platz.

In 1793 he went with his master
to the siege of Mainz. He continued
his optical studies during the bombardment, witnessed the marching out of the
garrison, and was one of the first to
enter the conquered town. He received
leave to withdraw, and went to his
mother at Frankfort, and persuaded her
to sell the old house and its contents,
and to provide a more convenient home
for her old age. There was some talk

of her coming to Weimar. In the
autumn of this year the duke left the
Prussian service, and Goethe could look
forward to a period of peace. He was
chiefly occupied with the management
of the theatre, and for this he wrote
two pieces, both of which had reference
to the politics of the time. The *Bürger-
general* is a satire on the Revolution,
and was long a rock of offence to
Goethe's friends, who thought that he
should have hailed with delight the
birth of a new era. The *Aufgeregten*,
left unfinished, sketched the outbreak of
the Revolution in a country town, and
would have declared the author's views
with greater distinctness. But the feelings of scorn and contempt which he felt
for the cowardice, cunning, and perfidy
of mankind were expressed in a work
of greater magnitude. He had good
reason to deplore the misery of the
time. His mother's home in Frankfort

was broken up ; Schlosser, his brother-in-law, had retired to Auerbach ; Jacobi was flying to Holstein. Goethe took the old German epic of *Reynard the Fox*, with which he had long been familiar, and which, under the guise of animals, represents the conflicting passions of men, and re-wrote it in flowing German hexameters.

Thus far he had produced but little since his return from Italy. He was now to undergo the most powerful influence which had as yet affected his life. His friendship with Schiller was now to begin, an alliance which, in the closeness of its intimacy and its deep effect on the character of both friends, has scarcely a parallel in literary history. If Schiller was not at this time at the height of his reputation, he had written many of the works which have made his name famous. He was ten years younger than Goethe. The *Räuber*

Friendship with Schiller.

plays the same part in his literary history as *Götz* plays in that of Goethe.
This had been followed by *Fiesco* and
Kabale und Liebe. The second period
of Schiller's life had begun with his
friendship with Körner, and his resi-
dence in Saxony. Here he wrote the
Hymn of Joy, and completed *Don
Carlos*. In 1787 he settled at Weimar.
He found the place deserted, the duke
in the Prussian camp, Goethe in Italy.
He applied himself to history, wrote the
Revolt of the Netherlands, and studied
the literature and art of Greece. In
1789, mainly upon Goethe's recom-
mendation, Schiller was made professor
of history at the University of Jena,
although he was afraid lest the scholars
should discover that they knew more
history than the teacher. Here he
made a successful marriage, and worked
seriously at his *History of the Thirty
Years' War*. In 1794 Schiller had

arranged with the publisher, Cotta of
Augsburg, whose name is from this
time indissolubly connected with the
history of German literature, for the
production of a new literary journal.
It was to be called the *Horen*, and the
most distinguished German writers were
to contribute to it. Goethe accepted
the invitation willingly. The work was
designed to mark an epoch in German
taste, and it did so. It soon had two
thousand subscribers. Among those
who promised to contribute were not
only Matthisson, Herder, Knebel, Fritz
Jacobi, and Gleim, but the brothers
Humboldt, the veteran Kant, the youthful Fichte, who had just begun to lec-
ture in Jena, and, at a later period, the
brothers Schlegel. Schiller opened the
first number of the journal with his
letters on the "Æsthetic Education of
the Human Race." Goethe contributed the "Unterhaltungen deutscher

Ausgewanderten," a series of stories told by a number of German emigrants who had been driven to cross the Rhine by the invasion of the French. The most remarkable of these stories is the " Märchen," a wild and mystic tale, which has been the subject of as much controversy and of as many interpretations as the second part of *Faust*. Goethe also published in the *Horen* the " Römische Elegien," the flavour of which even Karl August found a little too strong. The first effect of Schiller's influence on Goethe was the

Wilhelm Meister. completion of *Wilhelm Meisters Lehrjahre*. Goethe had conceived the plan of the work twenty years before, and the first six books had been written before the Italian journey. It was now finished by the addition of two more books. It stands in the first rank of Goethe's writings. His aim in it is to attain to perfect objectivity of tone, to represent men as they are, and to pass no judgment upon them. The hero passes with weak irresolution through a number of ordinary circumstances, apparently the sport of fortune and the plaything of chance, yet all these experiences have their definite result in the training of his character. Like the son of Kish, he goes forth to seek his father's asses and finds a kingdom. The unearthly charm of the child Mignon, the dark fate which shrouds the aged harper like the doom of Œdipus, the uncertain yearning after a happier home in brighter climes, give a deeper undertone to the prevailing lightness of the story. The style is exquisitely soft and flowing. It has the sweetness and simplicity of *Werther*, but is more mellow and more mature. The sixth book is occupied with the *Bekenntnisse einer schönen Seele*, a piece of the autobiography of Goethe's early friend Fräulein von Klettenberg,

H

altered to suit its new surroundings.
The *Musen Almanach* for 1796, edited
by Schiller, was enriched by some of
Goethe's most exquisite poems—*Die
Nähe des Geliebten, Meeres Stille,* and
Glückliche Fahrt. The storm of criticism which was aroused by the *Horen,*
and the little success which, after the
first numbers, it met with from the
public, determined the two friends to
retaliate upon their aggressors. The
poems of Martial contain a number of
epigrams written in two lines, describing
the numberless little presents or *xenia,*
which it was customary for friends to
exchange at Rome during the time of
Xenien. the Saturnalia. The name was borrowed by the two poets, and the *Xenien*
was a convenient vehicle for the expression of their opinion on every subject.
The newspapers of the day were the
first object of attack, but they soon
went farther afield. The epigrams were

written in Schiller's rooms at Jena.
It is impossible to fix the authorship of
the *Xenien;* one conceived the idea, the
other wrote the lines; one wrote the
hexameter, the other the pentameter;
they intended the authorship as well as
the ownership of the copyright to be
one and indivisible. Notwithstanding
this, the collection has been broken up.
There is no guarantee that the epigrams
which appear in the separate works of
either poet were really written by the
authors to whom they are ascribed;
some are reprinted in the works of
both; some have remained unprinted
altogether. They appeared in the
Musen Almanach for 1797, together
with the Venetian elegies mentioned
above. It is needless to say that they
roused the writers whom they attacked
to unspeakable fury, and were the occasion of a copious literature. A more
solid result of the friendship between

Hermann und Dorothea. the poets was the production of *Hermann und Dorothea.* It is a German idyll ; the story is taken from the sufferings of Lutherans driven out in the early part of the 18th century from the province of Salzburg, but Goethe has given it the character of his own time. He had seen much of the suffering produced by the French Revolution, and he wished this poem to be a reflexion in a tiny mirror of the storms and convulsions of the great world. In its literary form it is a descendant of Voss's *Luise.* It was conceived at Ilmenau in August, 1796, and finished in the following spring. Schiller tells us how it was composed with extraordinary ease and rapidity. During nine days Goethe produced 150 lines a day. You have only to shake the tree, as Schiller said, and ripe apples will tumble down about you. The lines thus hastily written underwent a careful revision. Contem-

poraneous with *Hermann und Dorothea*
is the production of *Wallensteins Lager*
by Schiller, which was written with the
advice and assistance of his brother
poet. The completion of this cycle of
plays falls two years later.

The year 1797 is the year of ballads. Ballads.
In his garden house at Jena, Schiller
worked diligently at this vein, that perhaps for which he was best suited, and
in which he most nearly rivals Goethe.
Goethe wrote *Die Braut von Korinth,*
Gott und die Bayadere, and *Der Zauber-*
lehrling; and the whole collection was
published in the *Musen Almanach* for
1798. The latter half of this year was
occupied with a tour in Switzerland.
Before its commencement he visited his
mother at Frankfort for the last time, and
presented to her his wife and his son.
It was a year of extraordinary activity.
Besides the ballads and the researches
in the morphology of plants and insects,

Goethe translated a great part of the
autobiography of Benvenuto Cellini,
wrote a number of essays on the ques-
tion of æsthetics, and worked at his long
neglected *Faust.* Of this he wrote the
dedication, the " Prologue in Heaven,"
and the " Golden Marriage of Oberon
and Titania "—so powerful was the effect
of intellectual sympathy and stimulus.

The six years which succeeded
Goethe's return from his third Swiss
tour, although they embrace the period
in which he and Schiller were in daily
co-operation, have left us little of permanent worth from the older poet.
On the other hand, they are the years
of Schiller's greatest activity. The
great trilogy of *Wallenstein,* perhaps
the highest point of Schiller's genius,
was followed by *Maria Stuart,* the
Jungfrau von Orleans, the *Braut von
Messina,* and *Wilhelm Tell.* From the
end of 1799 Schiller was permanently

settled in Weimar ; a dramatic school was founded, and the representation of these classical dramas was the glory of the Weimar stage. During these years Goethe was occupied with *Faust*, with his researches into the theory of colours and of biological development, with the conduct of the theatre and the practical enccuragement of Art. In 1798 the *Horen* died a natural death, and was succeeded by the *Propyläen*, a journal of literature and criticism, which, although it contained many essays by Goethe, never exceeded a circulation of 300. In the spring 1799 the study of Homer incited Goethe to sketch a long epic poem on the subject of Achilles. Schiller did his best to encourage the work. The first canto was rapidly completed, but it had no successor. Goethe contented himself with translating the works of others, and prepared the *Mahomet* and *Tancred* of Voltaire for the Leipsic stage.

In the first days of the new century
Goethe suffered from a dangerous attack
of scarlatina.   His friends feared for
his life.   Frau von Stein recalled her
forgotten friendship, and showed kindness to his son.   After his recovery he
sketched out what was the most important work of these years, a trilogy on
the subject of the French Revolution ;
of this only the first part, the *Natürliche
Tochter*, was completed.   The story was
a true one of a princess of the French
house of Conti.   The play is written
with the full beauty of Goethe's style,
and some passages and effects are
worthy of his highest genius.   But as
a whole it fails.   It has the quality,
which in a drama must be a fault, so
characteristic of Goethe's later writing,
of too great universality of treatment.
The characters are not living beings,
but abstractions ; and the language is
vague and general, rather than clear and

defined. The play was performed at Weimar on April 2, 1803. Two master-pieces of Schiller—the *Braut von Messina* and the *Jungfrau von Orleans*—preceded and followed it by a few weeks. At the end of this year Madame de Staël arrived in Weimar, accompanied by Benjamin Constant. She had heard of the fame of this new Parnassus, and she was bent on pro-claiming the intellectual superiority of Germany to the world. Goethe at first fled from her, as Byron did at a later period. He hid himself in Jena, but was recalled by order of the duke. The result of the conversations in the salons of Weimar is contained in her book *De l'Allemagne.* In March she was sud-denly recalled by the death of her father, the minister Necker. Goethe was at this time the centre to which the most distinguished men of all kinds in Ger-many naturally turned. He was most

Madame de Staël.

intimate with Zelter the musician, with
whom he maintained a full correspondence ; with Wilhelm von Humboldt,
the statesman-scholar ; with F. A. Wolf,
the founder of the science of philology ; with Gottfried Hermann, the best
authority on Greek metres.　But the
Schiller's friendship which was worth all these
death. was soon to be severed.　In the beginning of 1805 Goethe was convinced
that either he or Schiller would die in
that year.　In January they were both
seized with illness ; Schiller had finished
his *Phädra* and begun to work at his
Demetrius.　Goethe was translating the
Neveu de Rameau of Diderot.　Schiller
was the first to recover, and visiting
Goethe in his sick room, fell on his neck
and kissed him with intense emotion.
On April 29 they saw each other for
the last time.　Schiller was on his way
to the theatre, whither Goethe was too
ill to accompany him.　They parted at

the door of Schiller's house. Schiller died on the evening of the 9th of May. No one dared to tell Goethe the sad news, but he saw in the faces of those who surrounded him that Schiller must be very ill. On the morrow of Schiller's death, when his wife entered his room, he said, " Is it not true that Schiller was very ill yesterday ?" She began to sob. He then cried, " He is dead!" " Thou hast spoken it thyself," she answered. Once more he cried, " He is dead !" and turning aside covered his weeping eyes with his hands. Goethe at first intended to have completed *Demetrius* as a memorial of his friend, but a happier inspiration was to arrange a performance of Schiller's great poem of *The Bell*, and to crown it by an epilogue. Since that time Schiller and Goethe have been inseparable in the minds of their countrymen, and have reigned as twin stars in the literary

firmament. If Schiller does not hold
the first place, it is at least true that
he is more beloved, although Goethe
may be more admired. It would be
invidious to separate them. But it is
evident that the best fruits of Schiller's
muse were produced when he was most
closely under Goethe's influence, and
the foreign student of German culture
has ground for believing that at some
future time the glory of the lesser lumi-
nary will be absorbed in that of the
greater, and the name of Goethe will
represent alone and unrivalled the literature of his age and country.

Napoleon.   Schiller was happy in the occasion of
his death. He did not see the troubles
which immediately afterwards burst upon
Thuringia. On October 14, 1806, the
battle of Jena was fought. The court
had fled from Weimar ; only the duchess
Louise remained. In the evening of the
defeat Weimar was plundered by the

conquering troops. Many of Goethe's
friends lost everything they possessed.
His property and perhaps his life was
saved by the firmness of Christiane, and
afterwards by the billeting of Marshal
Augereau in his house. On the 15th
Napoleon entered the town, but Goethe
did not go to see him. The duchess
obtained her husband's pardon by her
entreaties. It was not till the autumn
of 1808 that Napoleon and Goethe,
perhaps the two greatest men then living
in Europe, met and conversed. It was
at the congress of Erfurt, where the
sovereigns and princes of Europe were
assembled. Goethe's presence was
commanded by the duke. He was attracted at least as much by the prospect
of seeing Talma as of meeting Napoleon.
He was invited to an audience on
October 2 ; Talleyrand, Berthier, and
Savary were present. The emperor sat
at a large round table eating his break-

fast. He beckoned Goethe to approach him, and said to him, "Vous êtes un homme!" He asked how old he was, expressed his wonder at the freshness of his appearance, said that he had read *Werther* through seven times, and made some acute remarks on the management of the plot. Then, after an interruption, he said that tragedy ought to be the school of kings and peoples ; that there was no subject worthier of treatment than the death of Cæsar, which Voltaire had treated insufficiently. A great poet would have given prominence to Cæsar's plans for the regeneration of the world, and shown what a loss mankind had suffered by his murder. He invited Goethe to Paris; that was the centre of great movements ; there he would find subjects worthy of his skill. They parted with mutual admiration. There were three portraits of Napoleon in Goethe's study.

In the same year, 1808, an edition of Faust. Goethe's works in thirteen volumes was published by Cotta at Tübingen. It is remarkable as containing the first part of *Faust* in its complete form. The principal portions of the drama had already been published as a fragment in 1790. It had then attracted but little attention. Heyne wrote of it—" There are fine passages in it, but with them there are such things as only he could give to the world who takes other men to be blockheads." Wieland and Schiller were apparently dissatisfied with it. It had perhaps the appearance of patch-work, as it was made up of fragments which had been written at very different periods of his life. The idea of writing *Faust* seems to have come to Goethe in his earliest manhood. He was brooding over it at the same time with *Götz von Berlichingen;* but at Strasburg he spoke to Herder ·of neither. He

apparently began to write it down at
the same time as *Werther* in 1774, and
we find mention of its progress in the
two following years ; indeed, all the
important parts of the fragment which
appeared in 1790 were known to Jacobi
before 1776. He took the work with
him to Italy, where he added little to it
except the scene in the witches' kitchen.
The dedication, the "Prologue in
Heaven," which presents to the reader
the idea of the whole work, the prelude
on the stage copied from the Indian
drama, the lyrical intermezzo, the scene
with Wagner before the city gate, and
the scene with Mephistopheles in the
study were written before 1800. In that
year he was busy with Helena for the
second part; and he added nothing afterwards to the first, except the "Walpurgis Night" and the scene of Valentine's
death. *Faust* justly stands at the head
of all Goethe's works, and it deserves a

very high place among the best works
of every age. Founded on a well-
known popular tale, indebted for its
interest and pathos to incidents of
universal experience, it deals with the
deepest problems which can engage the
mind of man. In this combination of
qualities it is perhaps superior to any
one of Shakespeare's plays. The plot
is as simple and as well known to the
audience as the plot of a Greek tragedy.
The innocence and fall of Gretchen appeal to every heart; the inward struggles of Faust, like those of Hamlet, and
the antagonism of the sensual and moral
principles, interest the reader just in
proportion as his own mind and nature
have been similarly stirred. Each line
is made to stand for eternity ; not a
word is thrown away ; the poem has
entered as a whole into the mind and
thought of modern Germany ; nearly
every expression has become a house-

I

hold word. Characters are sketched in
a single scene; Valentine lives for us as
clearly as Faust himself. Deeper mean-
ings are opened up at every reading,
and the next age will discover much in
it which is concealed from this. Goethe,
writing of *Faust* in his eightieth year,
says with truth, " The commendation
which the poem has received far and
near may be perhaps owing to this
quality, that it permanently preserves
the period of development of a human
soul which is tormented by all that
afflicts mankind, shaken also by all that
disturbs it, repelled by all that it finds
repellent, and made happy by all that it
desires. The author is at present far
removed from such conditions; the
world likewise has to some extent other
struggles to undergo; nevertheless the
state of man, in joy and sorrow, remains
very much the same, and the latest born
will still find cause to acquaint himself

with what has been enjoyed and suffered
before him in order to adapt himself to
that which awaits him."

In 1809 he finished *Die Wahlver-*
wandtschaften (The Elective Affinities),
a story which is always cited to prove
the immoral tendency of his works. A
married couple, Edward and Charlotte,
are thrown into constant companionship
with two unmarried persons, the Captain
and Ottilie. A cross attraction takes
place similar to that which is often seen
in chemical experiments. Edward
unites himself with Ottilie, Charlotte
with the Captain. The psychological
changes by which this result is produced are portrayed with a masterly
hand. The moral may be held by some
to exalt the preponderance of fatality in
human affairs, and the uselessness of
contending against irresistible circumstances. Others may believe that the
story is intended to show the disastrous

Wahlver-
wandt-
schaften.

calamities which may be wrought by a
weak and self-indulgent will. Ottilie,
though she cannot resist her passion,
has strength enough to starve herself to
death ; Edward is the prototype of
Arthur Donnithorne and Tito Melema.
The work is replete with earnest purpose and terrible warning.

Farben-
lehre.

    In 1810 Goethe finished the printing
of his *Farbenlehre* (Theory of colours),
a work which had occupied his mind
ever since his journey to Italy. His
theories were rejected and disregarded
by his contemporaries, but he left them
with confidence to the judgment of
posterity. Goethe's labours in this
domain fall into two natural divisions—
one in which he tries to prove that the
hypotheses of Newton are unsatisfac-
tory, and another, in which he promul-
gates a theory of his own. In his first
work, published in 1791 and 1792, he
describes with great accuracy and liveli-

ness the experiments which he has made. They consist chiefly of the appearances presented by white discs on a black ground, black discs on a white ground, and coloured discs on a black or white ground when seen through a prism. There are two points which he considers fatal to Newton's theory, — that the centre of a broad white surface remains white when seen through a prism, and that even a black streak on a white ground can be entirely decomposed into colours. The scientific friends to whom he communicated these observations assured him that there was nothing in them opposed to Newton's theory,—that they were even confirmations of it. He would not be convinced, and took no pains to acquire that exact knowledge of mathematics and geometrical reasoning without which the more abstruse problems of physical optics could not be intelligible. He went on further to

formulate a theory of his own. His
views on the subject are contained in
their shortest form in a letter addressed
to Jacobi from the camp at Marienburg,
in July, 1793. They are divided into
six heads, of which the following is an
abstract. (1) Light is the simplest
matter we have knowledge of, the least
capable of analysis, the most homo-
geneous. It is not a compound body.
(2) Least of all is it compounded of
coloured lights. Every coloured light
is darker than colourless light. Bright-
ness cannot be compounded of darkness.
(3) Inflexion, refraction, reflexion, are
three conditions under which we often
observe apparent colours, but they are
rather occasions for their appearance
than the cause of it. (4) There are
only two pure colours, blue and yellow ;
red may be regarded as a property of
both of them. There are two mixed
colours, green and purple ; the rest are

gradations of these colours, and are not pure. (5) Colourless light cannot be produced out of coloured lights, nor white from coloured pigments. (6) The colours which appear to us arise solely out of a modification of the light. The colours are excited in the light, not developed out of the light. These views he afterwards extended and explained, but very slightly modified. In Goethe's opinion, yellow was light seen through a thickened medium ; blue was darkness seen through an illuminated medium ; all other colours were derived from these two. The theory of the *Farbenlehre* has not yet received the recognition which Goethe anticipated for it. In his own day he had some adherents,—the most distinguished perhaps was the philosopher Hegel, whose views, however, of natural philosophy have caused some inquirers to recoil from his theory of metaphysics. Goethe complained

that no physicist believed in him, and as
that is still true in an age which has
been devoted more than any other to
physical inquiries, we may conclude that
the principle upon which his theories are
based is radically wrong.

The year 1809, in which *Die Wahl-
verwandtschaften* was written, was for
Goethe the beginning of a new era. He
was then fresher and brighter than he
had been for ten years before. He had
lived through a troubled period of op-
pressive sorrow. The death of Schiller,
the violation of his beloved Weimar,
the deaths of the duchess Amalia and of
his mother, his own bodily and mental
sufferings, had given a tone of sadness
to his poetry. As if to put the finishing
stroke to the efforts of his life, having
married the mother of his children, he
arranged and published his collected
works, and completed his theory of
colours. The unfinished drama of

Pandora is a symbol of this time. The part which is completed refers only to past experiences of sadness; the continuation was to have lifted the curtain of future hope.

It was natural, at the beginning of a new course of life, that Goethe should write an account of his past existence. The study of his collected poems made it apparent to him how necessary it was to furnish a key by which they might be understood. These various causes led to the composition of *Dichtung und Wahrheit* (Poetry and Truth), an autobiographical history of the poet's life from his birth till his settlement at Weimar. This work is the cause of much embarrassment to the poet's biographers. Where it ought to be the most trustworthy source of information, it is most misleading. It is probable that Goethe intended it to be an accurate and circumstantial account of his

Autobiography.

life. But the inner life of an individual
is more clear to him than the outer.
The s ges of our self-development are
better remembered than the exact circumstances which produced them, still
less than the order of time in which they
followed each other. Goethe took pains
to ascertain facts which he had forgotten.
But he was so conscious that imagination would play a large part in the composition, that in the title he gave Poetry
the precedence before Truth. The in-
defatigable industry of German inves-
tigation has laid open before us every
detail of the poet's life and every phase
of his feeling. *Dichtung und Wahrheit*,
if it has lost its rank as a history, still
keeps its place as a classic. The simple
loving delineation of the childhood of
genius is as fresh as ever, and is of
more universal interest from being less
particular. The first five books of this
autobiography appeared in 1811, the

next five in 1812, the third instalment
at Easter, 1814, and the conclusion after
Goethe's death.

The period during which this was his
principal work witnessed the greatest
political event of the first half of our
century, the rising of the German people
against the power of Napoleon. In this
Goethe took no share, and with it he apparently felt little sympathy. He made
no impassioned orations to his countrymen, like Fichte ; he wrote no inspiring
lays like Körner. The ballads which he
composed in 1813 are harmless enough,
—*Der wandelnde Glocke, Der getreue
Eckhart, Der Todtentanz.* He saw
Stein and Arndt at Dresden in 1813,
but disappointed them by his impassive
manner. He said to Körner's father at
the same time, " Yes, shake your chains !
The man is too great for you. You
will not break them, but only drive them
deeper into your flesh." The reasons

The war
of liber-
ation.

for this apparent coldness are perhaps
more simple than they appear at first
sight. Goethe was a man of thought
rather than of action. Although a fair
portion of his long life was given to the
practical business of his adopted country,
his heart was always in speculation or
artistic production. While inspecting
mines he was spinning theories of geo-
logical formation ; while working for the
War Commission he gladly ran away to
the castle of Dornburg to bury himself
amongst his deserted papers. The
pressure of court business at Weimar
drove him to the solitude of Italy. In
the defiles of the Argonne, and in the
trenches before Mainz, he was schem-
ing and arranging his theory of colours.
A bombardment was valued by him less
as an attack upon the enemy than as
a series of interesting experiments in
optics. Added to this natural indifference to the details of human affairs was

his belief in the predominance of force, and in the necessary evolution of the history of the world. Napoleon was to him the greatest living depository of power. Nations, whether conquered or victorious, separated or united, obeyed a common law against which individual will strove in vain. Goethe was thus incapacitated for politics, both by his qualities and his defects. This habit of abstract contemplation grew upon him in later life. Those who condemn him on this ground should remember that he hailed in no grudging spirit the formation of a united Germany, and that his works have been the most potent agency in making all Germans feel that they are one. Few would wish to exchange the self-conflict of *Faust*, or even the wayward wanderings of *Meister*, for the hectic extravagance of Körner or the unsubstantial rhetoric of Schiller's Posa.

It was hardly to be expected that at

the age of sixty-five Goethe should strike out new lines of poetical activity.

However, in the *West-östliche Divan*, he made the first attempt to transplant Eastern poetry to a German soil, and set an example which has been followed by Heine and Mirza Schaffy. In 1811 he first became acquainted with the works of Hafiz in Hammer's translation. At a time when North and South and West were splitting in sunder, when thrones were breaking up and empires trembling, he sought a willing refuge in the restoring fountain of the Eastern poet. The book *Timur* has an obvious reference to the expedition of Napoleon in Russia, but the large majority of the poems are amatory, and are addressed to an imaginary Suleika, whose name is given to one of the books. Once more, in his old age, Goethe came under the sovereignty of a woman. She was Marianne von Willemer, the newly married wife of

a Frankfort banker, Jacob von Willemer, who was an old friend of Goethe's
and of his brother-in-law Schlosser.
Goethe made her acquaintance in a
journey which he took in the Rhine
country with Sulpiz Boiserée, who had
succeeded in interesting Goethe in early
German Art, a subject to which he was
himself devoted. The correspondence
between Goethe and Marianne was published in 1877. It extends almost to
the day of his death, and includes letters
from Eckermann giving an account of
his last moments. Not only were most
of the *Divan* poems addressed to Suleika,
but several of those included in the collection are by Marianne herself, and will
bear comparison with those of Goethe.
In these poems the Oriental form is not
very strictly observed. The fondness of
the Orientals for the repetition of single
rhymes is not attended to, and if sometimes remembered is soon forgotten.

Their Eastern colour depends rather on
the suggestion of Eastern scenery and
the introduction of Eastern names.
This, however, gives the poet a greater
licence to levity, to fatalism, and to passion, than would have been possible in
poems of a purely German character.

The
closing
years.
The last twelve years of Goethe's life,
when he had passed his seventieth birthday, were occupied by his criticisms on
the literature of foreign countries, by the
Wanderjahre, and the second part of
Faust. He was the literary dictator of
Germany and of Europe. He took but
little interest in the direction in which
the younger German school was moving,
and was driven to turn his eyes abroad.
He conceived an intense admiration for
Byron, which was increased by his early
death. Byron appears as Euphorion in
the second part of *Faust.* Goethe also
recognised the greatness of Scott, and
was one of the first to send a greeting to

the Italian Manzoni.   He conceived the
idea of a world-literature transcending
the narrow limits of race and country,
which should unite all nations in harmony of feeling and aspiration.   German
writers claim that his design has been
realized, and the literature of every age
and country can be studied in a tongue
which Goethe had made rich, flexible,
and serviceable for the purpose.   The
Wanderjahre, although it contains some *Meister's*
of Goethe's most beautiful conceptions, *Wander-jahre.*
The Flight into Egypt, The Description
of the Pedagogic Province, The Parable
of the Three Reverences, is yet an ill-
assorted collection of all kinds of writings,
old and new.   Its author never succeeded in giving it form or coherency,
and his later style, beautiful as it is,
becomes in these years vague and
abstract.   Still, without this work we
should not be acquainted with the full
richness and power of Goethe's mind.

K

Second
part of
Faust.

The second part of *Faust* has been
a battlefield of controversy since its publication, and demands fuller attention.
Its fate may be compared with that of
the latest works of Beethoven. For a
long time it was regarded as impossible
to understand, and as not worth understanding, the production of a great artist
whose faculties had been impaired by age.
By degrees it has, by careful labour,
become intelligible to us, and the con-
viction is growing that it is the deepest
and most important work of the author's
life. Its composition cannot be called
an after-thought. There is no doubt
that the poet finished at the age of
eighty the plan which he had conceived
sixty years before. The work in its en-
tirety may be described as the first part
of *Faust* " writ large." This is a picture
of the macrocosm of society as the earlier
play was of the microcosm of the individual. The parallelism between the

two dramas is not perfect, but it reveals
itself more and more clearly to a patient
study. The first act, with its varied
scenes of country, castle, garden, gal-
leries, and halls, answers to the two
prologues of the first part; the second
act introduces us again to Faust's study
and his familiar Wagner. The classical
Walpurgis Night has its prototype in the
first part. The third act is devoted to
Helena, who is the heroine of the second
part as Gretchen is of the first. The
marriage of Faust and Helena typifies
the union of the classical and romantic
schools, and their child is Euphorion,
who is symbolical of Byron. In the
fourth act Faust is raised instead of
being degraded by his union with
Helena. He wishes for a sphere of
beneficent activity, and obtains it by
war. The fifth act is devoted to the
complete regeneration of the soul of
Faust. Even the sight of all that he

has accomplished does not satisfy him. It is not until he is blind to outward objects that one moment of divine rapture reveals to him the continuance of his work in coming generations, and convinces him that he has not lived in vain. In this one moment of supreme happiness he dies. The struggle for the possession of Faust's soul, indicated in the first part, is fully elaborated in the second. Mephistopheles is shown to have worked out the good in spite of himself, and Margaret appears trans-figured as the revelation to man of the divine love.

With the completion of *Faust* Goethe felt that the work of his life was ac-complished. He still continued to work with regularity. He ordered and arranged his writings, he laboured at his *Tages- und Jahresheften*, an auto-biographical journal of his life. He bated not one jot of heart or hope,

and took the liveliest interest in every
movement of literature and science.
When the news of the July Revolution
of 1830 reached Weimar, Goethe was
excited beyond his wont, not on account
of the triumph of liberal principles, but
because the controversy between Cuvier
and Geoffroy St. Hilaire had been decided in favour of the latter. Still he
had much to darken his latter days.
His old friends were falling fast around
him. His wife had died in 1816, after
a union of thirty years. He felt her loss
bitterly. The duchess Amalia had died
eight years before, not long after the
death of his own mother. He now had
to undergo sadder experiences when
he was less able to bear them. Frau
von Stein, with whom he had renewed
his friendship if not his love, died in
January, 1827 ; and in June, 1828, he lost
the companion of his youth, the grand-
duke Karl August, who died suddenly,

away from Weimar, on his return from
a journey. Goethe received the news
with outward calmness, but said fore-
bodingly, " Now it is all over," and went
to mourn and labour at the castle of
Dornburg, where everything reminded
him of the days of their early friendship.
The duchess Louise survived her husband till February, 1830. When Goethe
died in 1832 none of the old Weimar set
were left except Knebel, who lived two
years longer. A greater blow than these
was the death of his only son, whom, in
spite of his moral weakness, his father
deeply loved. He died at Rome, in
October, 1830, and is buried close by the
pyramid of Caius Cestius, where Goethe
himself once desired to be laid. We
have a full account of the last nine years
of Goethe's life from the writings of
Eckermann, who became his secretary
in 1823, lived with him till his death,
and has noted down his conversations

and his habits with the minuteness and
fidelity of a Boswell.

We must pass on to the closing scene. His
On Thursday, March 15, 1832, he spent death.
his last cheerful and happy day. He
was visited by the grand-duchess and
other friends. He awoke the next
morning with a chill. From this he
gradually recovered, and on Monday
was so much better that he designed to
begin his regular work on the next day.
But in the middle of the night he woke
up with a deathly coldness, which extended from his hands over his body,
and which it took many hours to subdue.
It then appeared that the lungs were
attacked, and that there was no hope of
his recovery. Goethe did not anticipate
death. He sat fully clothed in his
arm-chair in his tiny bedroom, made
attempts to reach his study, spoke con-
fidently of his recovery, and of the
walks he would take in the fine April

days.   His daughter - in - law Ottilie
tended him faithfully.   On the morning
of the 22nd his strength gradually left
him.   He sat slumbering in his arm-
chair, holding Ottilie's hand.   Her name
was constantly on his lips.   His mind
occasionally wandered, at one time to
his beloved Schiller, at another to a fair
female head with black curls, some passion of his youth.   His last words were
an order to his servant to open the
second shutter to let in more light.
After this he traced with his forefinger
letters in the air.   At half-past eleven
in the day he drew himself, without any
sign of pain, into the left corner of his
arm-chair, and went so peacefully to
sleep that it was long before the watchers
knew that his spirit was really gone.
He is buried in the grand-ducal vault,
where the bones of Schiller are also laid.

Goethe differs from all other great
writers, except perhaps Milton, in this

respect, that his works cannot be understood without a knowledge of his life,
and that his life is in itself a work of art,
greater than any work which it created.
This renders a long and circumstantial
biography a necessity to all who would
study the poet seriously. At the same
time he is so great that we are even
now scarcely sufficiently removed from
him to be able to form a correct judgment of his place in literary history.
He is not only the greatest poet of
Germany ; he is one of the greatest
poets of all ages. Posterity must decide
his exact precedence in that small and
chosen company which contains the
names of Homer, Dante, and Shakespeare. He was the apostle of self-
culture. Always striving after objective
truth, and sometimes attaining to it, he
exhibited to the world every phase of
his plastic mind in turn, and taught both
by precept and example the husbandry

of the soul. The charge of selfishness, so often brought against him, cannot be maintained. His nature responded to every influence of passing emotion. Like a delicate harp, it was silent if not touched, and yet gave its music to every wooing of the wilful wind. The charge of unsympathetic coldness roused the deep indignation of those who knew him best. He learned by sad experience that the lesson of life is to renounce. Rather than cavil at his statuesque repose, we should learn to admire the self-conflict and self-command which moulded the exuberance of his impulsive nature into monumental symmetry and proportion. His autobiography has done him wrong. It is the story, not of his life, but of his recollections. He needs no defence, nothing but sympathetic study. As Homer concentrated in himself the spirit of Antiquity, Dante of the Middle Ages, and Shakespeare of the Renaissance, so Goethe is the representative of the modern spirit, the prophet of mankind under new circumstances and new conditions, the appointed teacher of ages yet unborn.

BIBLIOGRAPHICAL SKETCH.

A COMPLETE bibliography of Goethe literature would fill a good-sized book, but it may be useful to indicate some of the principal sources of information about the poet without any attempt at an exhaustive statement. The most important authority for his life is his own work. The *Wahrheit und Dichtung*, the *Italienische Reise*, especially in its original form of letters to Frau von Stein, the *Reise am Rhein*, and the *Tages- und Jahresheften*, have an especial autobiographical value. German research has fixed the date and occasion of nearly all Goethe's poems, and there are few of them which do not help to illustrate his life. Of late years a complete catalogue of all Goethe's extant letters has been published, and a chronological record of all his reported conversations. The treasures of the Goethe *Haus* at Weimar have revealed much with regard to the poet, and will reveal more. With the help of diaries, sketches for finished works, the correspondence of friends, and other materials, we may be able to examine with correctness the whole working life of Goethe as it passed day by day. The spirit of order and punctuality which he inherited from his father is seen in the arrangement of his papers ; even his visiting cards were carefully preserved in chronological order. For the first period of Goethe's life *Der Junge Goethe*, in three volumes, published by Hirzel, with an introduction by Michael Bernays, is indispensable. It contains his letters and poems in chronological order. Among the letters of Goethe which have been published up to the last few years, are those to Schiller, Klopstock, Lavater, Zelter, Bettina von Arnim, Schulz, Countess Stolberg, Schlegel, Frau von Stein and her son Fritz von Stein, Jacob, his Leipzig friends, Reinhard, Knebel, Grüner, Herder, the Duke Karl August, F. A. Wolf, Johanna Fallmer, Marianne von Willemer, K. Göttling and Carlyle.

The first life of Goethe was published by Döring in 1828, of which a second enlarged edition appeared after the poet's death in 1833. Then followed the life by Viehoff, in four volumes, 1847–1853. A very excellent life is that of Schäfer, which appeared first in 1851, the third edition of which dates from 1871. It is contained in two volumes of moderate size, and is written with scarcely a superfluous word. The life by Düntzer (1880) is a most laborious and conscientious work : it narrates with precision every event of Goethe's life, but

is rather deficient in criticism.   It has been translated into English by T. W. Lyster, 1883.   We
should also mention *Goethe, sein Leben und seine
Werke*, by the Jesuit, Alexander Baumgartner, the
second edition of which was published in 1885.
It is a severe, and a somewhat unfair, criticism of
Goethe's life and works from the Catholic point of
view.   But it is well written, with full knowledge,
and is worth reading as showing everything that
may be urged against the character and genius of
the poet.   The account of Goethe and Schiller by
Karl Goedeke in his *Grundriss der deutschen Dichtung*, is admirable, and so is the little book *Goethe's
Leben und Schriften*, published by him in 1874.
The life of Goethe has been popularized in England
by G. H. Lewes in a work which has been as much
read in the German translation as in the original.
It is admirably written ; but while it deals adequately
with the main facts of Goethe's life, and his principal
works, it leaves many things untouched which a
biographer ought to notice.   The knowledge of
Goethe's works in England is due as much as
anything else to the writings of Thomas Carlyle.
Among the editions of Goethe's works the most
complete is that of Hempel, of which a new edition
is in course of publication.   The Commentaries of
Düntzer are also worthy of our praise ; they have

left no side of Goethe's activity and no period of his life unexplored. The new edition of Goethe's works, published under the auspices of the Duchess of Saxe-Weimar, in which all the treasures of the Goethe archives at Weimar will be printed, will supersede all others and form a fresh basis for criticism. We must not pass over the brilliant lectures on Goethe by Hermann Grimm, and the information given in the *Jahrbücher* of the German Goethe Society.

Translations of most of Goethe's works have been published in Bohn's Standard Library. The best translations of *Faust* into English are those of A. Hayward, John Anster, Theodore Martin, and Bayard Taylor. A translation of *Götz von Berlichingen*, by Sir Walter Scott, was published in 1799. Carlyle's translation of *Wilhelm Meister* is admirable in style and correctness.

A chronological list of the works of Goethe, published in his lifetime, is subjoined.

Von deutscher Baukunst	1773	*Erwin und Elmire*	1775
Götz von Berlichingen	1773	*Stella*	1776
Die Leiden des jungen		*Claudine von Villa*	
Werthers	1774	*Bella*	1776
Götter, Helden und		*Die Fischerinn*	1782
Wieland	1774	*Rede bei der Eröffnung*	
Neueröffnetes morali-		*des neuen Bergbaus*	
sches politisches		*zu Weimar*	1784
Puppenspiel	1774	*Die Vögel*	1787